Organ
TRANSPLANTS

ABDO
Publishing Company

Medical
Marvels

Organ
TRANSPLANTS

by Racquel Foran

Content Consultant

Susan Lederer
Robert Turell Professor of Medical
History and Bioethics
University of Wisconsin–Madison

Credits

Published by ABDO Publishing Company, PO Box 398166, Minneapolis, MN 55439. Copyright © 2014 by Abdo Consulting Group, Inc. International copyrights reserved in all countries. No part of this book may be reproduced in any form without written permission from the publisher. The Essential Library™ is a trademark and logo of ABDO Publishing Company.

Printed in the United States of America,
North Mankato, Minnesota
062013
092013

THIS BOOK CONTAINS AT LEAST 10% RECYCLED MATERIALS.

Editor: Arnold Ringstad
Series Designer: Craig Hinton

Photo credits: Sebastian Kaulitzki/Shutterstock Images, cover; Shutterstock Images, cover, 17, 19; Kevin Curtis/Science Photo Library/Getty Images, 7; Kathy Johnson/Courier News/AP Images, 10; Steve Helber/AP Images, 12; Matthias Schrader/Picture-Alliance/DPA/AP Images, 15; John Bazemore/AP Images, 22; Prakash Singh/AFP/Getty Images, 25; Universal History Archive/Getty Images, 28; NYPL/ScienceSource/Getty Images, 31; George F. Mobley/National Geographic/Getty Images, 34; Bettmann/Corbis/AP Images, 37, 98; Jack Sheahan/The Boston Globe/Getty Images, 39; Siri Mills/Newscom, 43; Keystone-France/Gamma-Keystone/Getty Images, 45; AP Images, 47, 52; Press Association/AP Images, 55; Fred Squillante/Columbus Dispatch/AP Images, 56; Soeren Stache/DPA/Picture-Alliance/Newscom, 62; Sal Veder/AP Images, 65; Sam Yu/Frederick News-Post/AP Images, 69; Forrest Anderson/AP Images, 71; AFP/Getty Images, 75; Duane R. Miller/AP Images, 76; Tsugufumi Matsumoto/AP Images, 85; The Times/Gallo Images/Getty Images, 87; University of Maryland Medical Center/AP Images, 89; Marijan Murat/Picture-Alliance/DPA/AP Images, 91; Sam Panthaky/AFP/Getty Images, 92 ; AOU Careggi Hospital/AP Images, 95; Oliver Sved/Shutterstock Images, 97

Library of Congress Control Number: 2013932976

Cataloging-in-Publication Data

Foran, Racquel.
 Organ transplants / Racquel Foran.
  p. cm. -- (Medical marvels)
Includes bibliographical references and index.
ISBN 978-1-61783-904-7
1. Transplantation of organs, tissues, etc.--Juvenile literature. I. Title.
617.9/5--dc23

2013932976

Contents

A New Heart

In 1998, Jessica Melore was an active 16-year-old. She was a captain of her high school tennis team, and she dreamed of attending Princeton University after graduation. But in one night, everything changed. During a family celebration, she became dizzy and experienced sharp pains in her chest, neck, and arms. She was rushed to the hospital, where doctors discovered she had suffered a massive heart attack. The prognosis was not good.

It was a shocking turn of events in young Jessica's life. A blood clot had become lodged in the artery leading to the left side of her heart. The surgeons were able to remove the clot, but her condition worsened. Doctors then attempted another surgery, but her lungs began to fill with liquid. A priest was brought in to read her last rites, a religious ritual performed as a person is dying. But

The marvel of modern organ transplants has extended the lives of thousands of people around the world.

The Power of Donation

Jessica received her heart from a young woman named Shannon Eckert who was killed in a car accident. Shannon's final selfless act changed the lives of several people. Her pancreas went to a 51-year-old man, her right kidney saved a 49-year-old man, her liver was donated to a 48-year-old, and another recipient received her corneas. Shannon's mother, Tammy, met Jessica in 2010.

Jessica was a fighter, and soon her condition stabilized. Still, her ordeal was far from over. Complications led to a loss of circulation in one of her legs. It became infected and had to be amputated just above the knee.

Doctors informed Jessica and her family a heart transplant was the only thing that could save her life. But donor hearts are not plentiful, and time was running out. To keep Jessica alive, doctors implanted a left ventricular assist device (LVAD) into her abdomen. An LVAD takes over the job of pumping for the left side of a damaged heart. It is connected to a battery pack worn outside the body. Jessica relied on the LVAD for nine long months. Finally, four days before her high school graduation, the telephone rang with news: a donor heart had become available.

Although the heart transplant process often involves a long wait, things must move very quickly as soon as a heart becomes available. A donor heart remains viable for only a short period of time. To preserve it during transportation, doctors must flush the heart with a cooling solution. They only have between four and six hours to move a heart out of the donor's body and into the recipient's. If any more time passes, the heart becomes too damaged to use.

The transplant surgery is complicated, but even more worrisome is the possibility of infection or rejection that exists after surgery. But Jessica's surgery was a success, and her body's immune system did not reject the organ. In 2003, she graduated from Princeton University with a degree in psychology. She then started working with the New Jersey Organ and Tissue-Sharing Network, a nonprofit donation group. Her incredible story would not have happened if not for the trailblazing doctors and surgeons who made heart transplants possible.

There were 2,348 heart transplant surgeries performed in the United States the year Jessica suffered her heart attack; 1,802 were performed in 2008.[1]

A Short History

By the time Jessica was rolled into surgery in 1999 to receive her new heart, transplant surgeons had amassed decades of human-to-human organ transplant experience. Organ transplantation shifted from crude experimentation to a viable medical option in less than 100 years.

In the late 1800s, disfigured soldiers were given crude skin transplants. In the early 1900s, blind patients were given sight again with cornea transplants. And by the 1950s, kidney transplants were saving patients' lives. After the success of kidney transplants, researchers were convinced it was medically possible to successfully transplant many of the body's organs, even the heart.

The medical advances that had to occur for organ transplants to be possible—from Alexis Carrel mastering the technique of connecting blood vessels in the early 1900s to the first successful human-to-human heart transplant in 1967—were vast and complex. The century-long history of modern transplant surgery can be divided into three phases: the research phase, the early clinical phase, and the modern era.

✚ New Ideas

Hundreds of years ago, challenging established scientific and medical beliefs and practices could result in severe punishment or even death. In the 1500s, a Spanish man named Miguel Serveto was burned at the stake after one of his works of religious criticism happened to note lung circulation seemed to be separate from the rest of the body's circulatory system. It is easy to understand why some might have resisted sharing their research and discoveries in the early days of medicine.

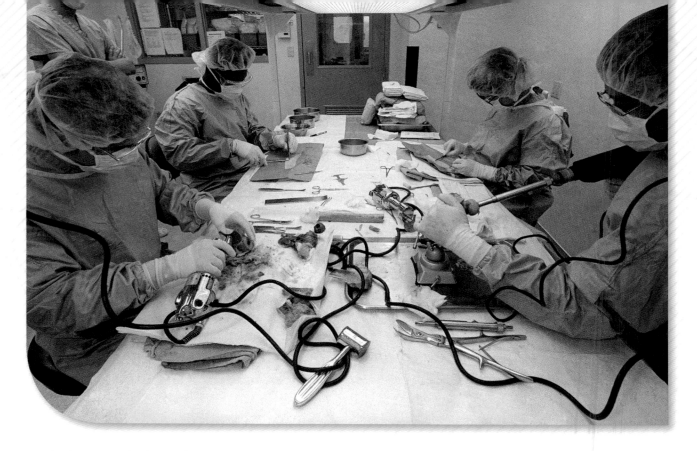

In the research phase, doctors began to understand how the body's organs work to keep people alive. They also discovered the ways in which the organs rely on each other to do their jobs. During the early clinical phase, pioneering surgeons began to actually test their ideas, first on animals and later on people. The challenges they faced led to the modern era, when the problem of organ rejection

Every year, transplant researchers make new discoveries that can extend the lives of patients around the world.

Recovery from heart transplant surgery can be relatively quick; some patients are up and walking within a few days and are home within two weeks.

was tackled. The modern era also brought about incredible advances in both mechanical organs and new organs created from patients' own cells.

The history tells of doctors willing to go to great lengths to advance the medical field and save the lives of men, women, and children. The risks, discoveries, and rewards these researchers experienced make the road to organ transplantation one of medicine's most fascinating journeys.

2

The Body's Organs

The human body is a very complex machine. It includes more than 7,500 named parts, including several dozen organs divided between 11 major organ systems.[1] All of these parts and systems must be strong and working together properly in order for humans to stay healthy. A single broken part can have a catastrophic domino effect on the entire body leading to the failure of an entire organ system. If not treated, a patient with a failing organ system could die.

An organ is a collection of tissues that work together to serve a specific body function. For example, the heart's function is to pump blood through the body. Organs rely on each other to serve their functions. For example, the heart pumps blood to the rest of the body, but it cannot function unless it is also supplied with blood itself. Blood provides nutrients to the entire body, but it can only

Modern science has helped doctors penetrate the mysteries of the enormously complex human body.

do so with the help of the heart pumping it through the blood vessels. And blood vessels cannot survive without the blood they are moving.

Transplantable Organs

Not all organs are transplantable today. The heart, lungs, kidneys, liver, and pancreas are the major organs that are commonly transplanted. Researchers are working to increase the size of this list. Still, the ability to transplant these few organs saves thousands of lives every year.

The heart, a hollow muscle roughly the size of a clenched fist, is the centerpiece of the circulatory system. It pumps blood through the blood vessels, which deliver oxygen and nutrients throughout the body. It circulates blood from its chambers to every cell in the body in less than a minute. A healthy heart beats anywhere from 60 to 100 times per minute. In a single day, it beats approximately

Spare Parts

Several body parts are no long considered vital to our existence. They are called vestigial organs. Once useful, evolution and changes in lifestyles have replaced or eliminated their functions but left the structures in place. The list includes the tailbone, wisdom teeth, and the appendix. Today, approximately 8 percent of people have their appendix removed with no ill effects.[2] However, in some plant-eating vertebrates, it remains part of the digestive system.

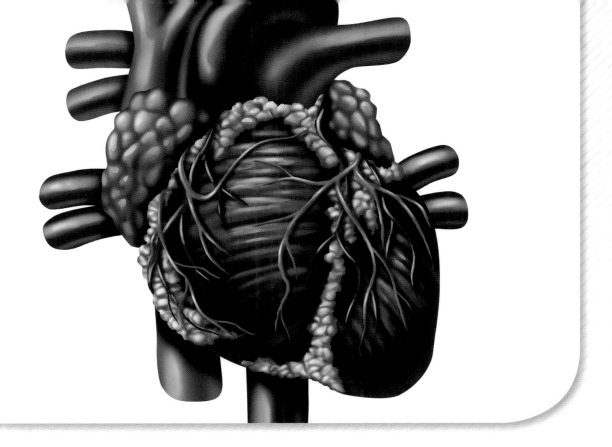

100,000 times, pumping 2,000 gallons (7,600 L) of blood a total distance of 60,000 miles (97,000 km).[3] Blocked blood vessels or a weakened heart are typical heart problems. A major heart attack, like the one Jessica Melore suffered, can damage the heart to the point where the only hope for the patient is a heart transplant.

Kidney Transplants

Since the body relies on the kidneys to filter all of its blood, kidney failure can cause a fatal buildup of chemicals in the bloodstream. In the event this happens, there are only two options: mechanical blood filtration in a process called dialysis or a kidney transplant. Kidney transplants are among the most common transplant operations performed, with approximately 17,000 performed in the United States in 2011.[5]

The lungs are two large organs in the chest. Their job is to add oxygen to the blood and remove carbon dioxide. When air is breathed in, the oxygen enters the lungs and travels through narrower and narrower tubes arranged in a branchlike structure until it reaches tiny air sacs called alveoli. Here, oxygen enters the blood, and carbon dioxide is removed. The lungs also serve to remove extra water from the body. Approximately one quart (0.95 L) of water leaves the body through normal breathing in a single day.[4] Though the two lungs look identical at first glance, the left lung is actually slightly smaller due to the off-center location of the heart nearby. People can live with just one lung, but their stamina will be decreased significantly.

The kidneys are a major component of an organ system known as the renal system. One of the system's key functions is to eliminate waste from the body through urine. The kidneys filter the blood, removing a chemical called

The kidneys can filter 160 quarts (150 L) of fluid each day. The red vessels contain oxygen-rich blood; the blue ones contain blood with less oxygen.

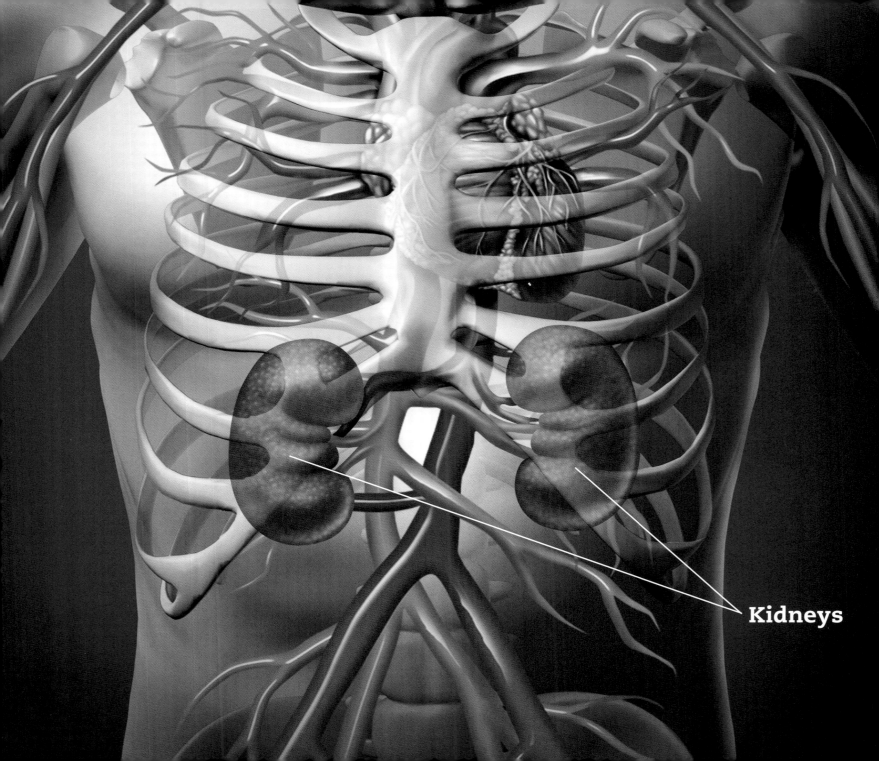

Kidneys

Liver Disease

Several diseases can cause liver damage, including cancer, cirrhosis, and hepatitis C. Alcohol, medicine, and viruses can all lead to cirrhosis, a disease in which scar tissue replaces healthy liver tissue, decreasing liver function. Hepatitis C is a blood infection that is caught when a person's blood comes into contact with an infected person's blood. Unlike the kidneys, a damaged liver cannot be replaced with machines. The only way to save the life of someone with a failing liver is to perform a transplant. A liver, however, is difficult to transplant because it is a very large organ and the liver is particularly sensitive to being cut off from a blood supply.

urea. Within the kidneys, tiny structures called nephrons are responsible for the filtering process. An average human kidney contains more than 1 million nephrons.[6] The nephrons filter all of the water in the body's blood every 45 minutes. The waste is then sent to the bladder to be removed from the body entirely. Bean-shaped, the kidneys are located in the lower abdomen. A person can live with just one kidney, making kidney donation an option for living patients with two healthy organs.

The liver is the body's largest internal organ. Shaped like a wedge, the versatile organ sits near the middle of the abdomen, below the heart. The liver creates a digestive fluid called bile, which both digests fats and removes waste from the blood. In addition to fats, the liver also helps process proteins and sugars from food into forms the body can use. The liver helps regulate the total volume of blood in the body, playing a part in the creation of fresh blood and in the destruction of old blood cells. When the liver is damaged, wastes and toxins can build up in the body, causing significant harm.

Another transplantable organ involved in the digestive system is the pancreas. It is a pear-shaped organ situated below the stomach. The pancreas creates chemicals that help the body break down food. It also releases chemicals to control the body's blood sugar level.

Injury, disease, age, poor diet, weight gain, and genetic abnormalities can lead to the breakdown of these systems. When any component of these systems breaks down, medical intervention is needed. In some cases, medication can fix the problem, but in other cases surgery is necessary. In extreme cases, an organ transplant may be required.

The Organ Transplant Process

Transplant surgery is extremely complex. It often involves more than a dozen medical professionals working upwards of 12 hours to remove the organ from the donor and then transplant it into the recipient. Each surgery is different depending on the organ being transplanted, but there are many common elements to the procedures.

When organ recipient patients arrive at the hospital they are prepared for surgery. They are given a sedative and intravenous tubes are inserted for delivering medications and fluids. Once the patient

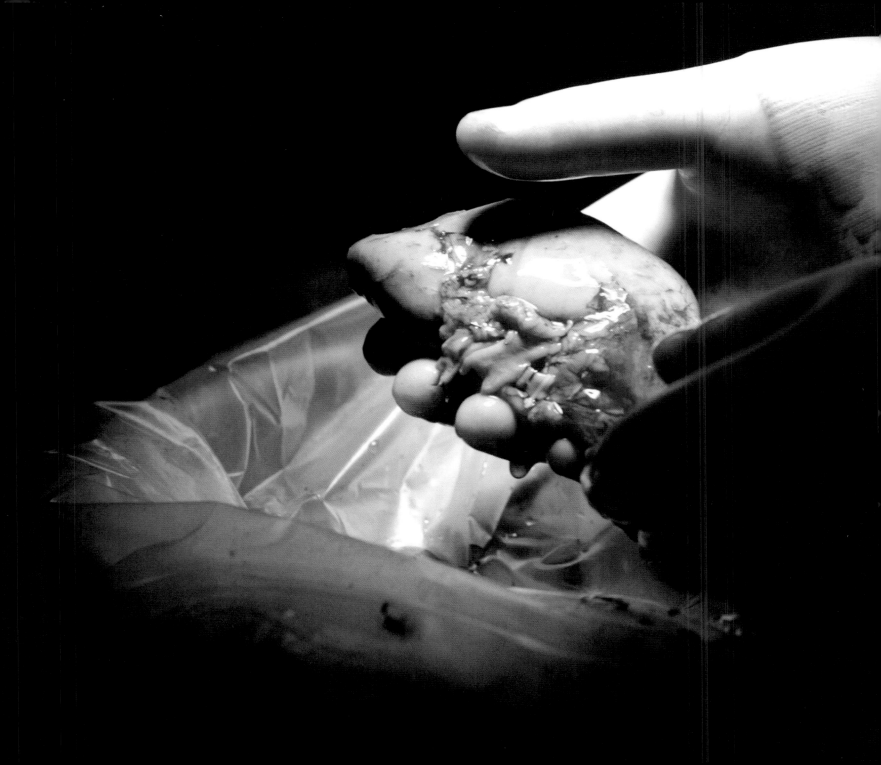

is ready, he or she is brought to the operating room. There, an anesthesiologist administers general anesthetic to render the patient unconscious. A central venous catheter, also called a central line, is then inserted in the arm, groin, or chest through the skin into a large vein. It is threaded through this vein until it reaches a large vein near the heart. This long, thin, flexible tube is used to provide the patient with medicines, fluids, nutrients, or blood products. A breathing tube is placed in the patient's throat and attached to a mechanical ventilator that expands the lungs during surgery. Then the patient is connected to a heart-lung bypass machine. The bypass machine does the job of the heart and lungs during the surgery. Finally, a nasogastric tube is put in place to drain stomach fluids, and a urinary catheter is inserted to drain urine during the surgery.

The patient is now ready for the surgeon to make the first incision. The size and location of the incision depends on the organ being transplanted. For a double lung transplant, the incision will be made horizontally across the chest below the breasts. The incision for a liver transplant is made in the upper abdomen. And for a kidney transplant, the incision is made in the lower right area of the torso. The patient's diseased organ is removed and the new organ gently put in place. Each blood vessel of the donor organ must then be sutured to the recipient's blood vessels to allow for blood flow to the transplanted organ. Developing these complex procedures and technologies was a long and difficult process for the many scientists and doctors involved. Their accumulated decades of work have saved thousands of lives around the world.

A doctor holds a donor kidney during a transplant surgery in 2008.

3

The Early History of Organ Transplants

Although the frequency and success rate of organ transplants has improved most dramatically over the last 50 years, the journey to successful transplantation has taken more than 5,000 years in all. Ancient Indian texts from as early as 3000 BCE describe skin grafting techniques. Surgeons performed nose reconstructions on prisoners whose noses had been mutilated as punishment for a crime. They used a flap of skin from the prisoner's forehead to rebuild the nose. In doing so, they discovered a key element for a successful transplant: skin tissue could survive only if the transplanted skin continued to have blood flowing through it.

Human organ transplantation was first described as a medical procedure in the writings of the Chinese scholar Liezi, who worked in approximately 400 BCE. The writings claim legendary Chinese

An exhibit in a New Delhi, India, museum shows what surgery might have looked like thousands of years ago.

> A transplant is also called a graft. Both the idea of organ transplantation and the terms *graft* and *transplant* were borrowed from horticulture. The technique of transplanting sections of plants to generate new plants has long been practiced.

physician Bian Qiao swapped the hearts of two soldiers in an effort to restore each man's health. According to the text both men survived. Although most consider this story to be myth, it does indicate how, early in human history, transplantation was considered a possible solution to bodily ailments.

It would be nearly 2,000 years before science began catching up to these forward-thinking ideas. In the late 1500s, an Italian surgeon named Gaspare Tagliacozzi used a technique similar to the one used by the Indian surgeon to restore the nose. Using the arm as a source of skin, his technique required his patients to walk around with their arm attached to their nose until the transplanted tissue grew its own blood supply and could then be severed from the arm. Tagliacozzi was also one of the first to note tissue could not be transplanted between two individuals. Modern science now knows immune system responses to foreign objects are the real reason for the difficulty in transplanting tissue between different people.

These early surgeries provided researchers with important information about what kept transplanted tissue viable. However, many more important discoveries had to be made before patients could expect successful organ transplants.

Blood Transfusions

Until surgeons found a way to replace lost blood, severe wounds were almost always deadly due to excessive blood loss. As early as the mid-1600s, scientists were experimenting with transferring blood from one animal to another to replace lost blood. It was not until the early 1800s that the first successful human-to-human blood transfusion was performed.

In 1818, Dr. James Blundell of Guy's Hospital in London, England, was called to help a woman who was bleeding severely after giving birth. Blundell had been experimenting on dogs for several years and had already discovered three

+ Discovering How Blood Flows

William Harvey was the first to recognize that blood flows quickly around the human body, being pumped through a single system of arteries and veins. Prior to this, physicians believed blood was used up by the body as it was produced, rather than circulating through blood vessels. They also thought two separate sets of vessels carried blood—one for nutrients from the liver and one for a then-unknown life-giving substance from the lungs. Although he likely made his discovery in 1618 or 1619, Harvey did not publish his findings until 1628. Because it was a major shift in thinking at the time, Harvey armed himself with many experimental results and supporting arguments to back up the idea.

important things. First, blood did not lose any of its properties when it passed through a syringe. Second, there is no significant difference between blood in the veins and blood from the arteries. And third, patients can survive small amounts of air in injected blood. He decided to perform a blood transfusion on the dying woman. Two ounces (0.06 L) of blood were transferred from her husband to her, and she recovered.

The fact that Dr. Blundell succeeded, however, was the result of luck. Dr. Blundell went on to perform ten more transfusions, but only half were successful. Blood types—the reason for incompatible blood between people—had not yet been discovered. It was not until 1901 that Karl Landsteiner discovered not all blood is the same and giving people the wrong blood type essentially poisons them. Once this discovery was made, doctors started matching patients' blood type to the donor blood for consistently successful transfusions. Now blood

Dr. Blundell published an article about a device used to transfer blood from one person to another in 1829.

The Heart-Lung Machine

If not for the invention of the heart-lung machine, open-heart surgery of any kind would not be possible. In order to perform successful heart surgery, oxygenated blood must continue to circulate throughout the body while the heart is being operated upon. In the early 1950s, US surgeon John H. Gibbon Jr. built the first heart-lung machine to provide artificial circulation. On May 6, 1953, this machine was used for 27 minutes when doctors repaired a hole in the heart of an 18-year-old girl. The machine was bulky and relatively primitive compared to today's technology, but for the first time surgeons could perform corrective surgery on an open heart.

transfusions are a common and often lifesaving part of many surgeries.

The ABO Blood Typing System

There are four major human blood types: A, B, AB, and O. Each has a different arrangement of antigens, foreign substances that cause an immune system response, and antibodies, the substances that fight antigens. Group A includes the A antigen and the B antibody, while Group B has the reverse—the B antigen and the A antibody. Group AB has both the A and B antigens but neither the A nor the B antibody. Finally, Group O has neither A nor B antigens, but does have both the A and B antibodies. These differing types are part of what makes blood transfusions and organ transplants so challenging.

Anesthesia

Discovering a safe way to replace blood lost during surgery brought surgeons one step closer to human organ transplants, but the patients themselves still stood in the way. Prior to the mid-1800s, patients who had to go under the surgeon's knife were strapped to a board and given a strong dose of alcohol to dull their senses. Still, they felt excruciating pain. Both the patient and the doctor had to have nerves of steel to go through with surgery.

The introduction of anesthetics for painkilling purposes drastically changed surgical practice. In the spring of 1842, Crawford Long was the first person to administer gas for surgical pain relief when he gave ether to a patient before removing a tumor from his neck. Four years

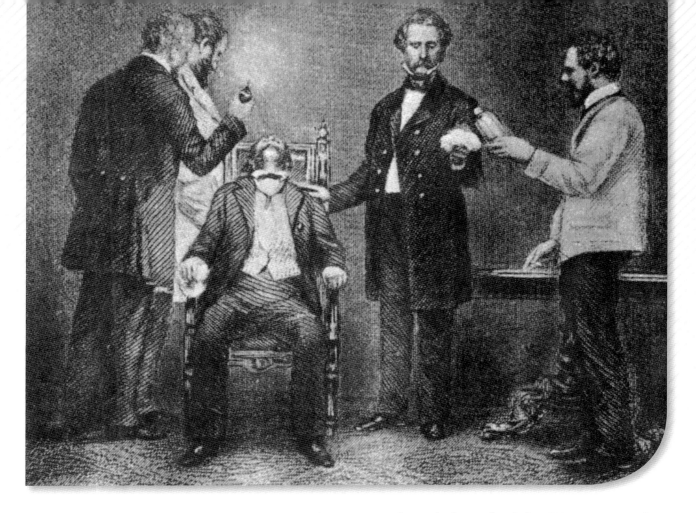

later, the first public display of surgical anesthesia was performed when John Collins Warren removed a tumor from the jaw of a patient after William Morton administered ether. Warren later wrote "[the patient] did not experience any pain at the time, although aware that the operation was proceeding."[1]

Antiseptic

Despite being able to operate on an unconscious patient, surgeons in the mid-1800s still lost as many patients as they saved. One of the most common reasons for death after surgery was infection, the introduction of disease-causing bacteria into surgical wounds. British surgeon and medical scientist Joseph Lister introduced the idea of antiseptic medicine. He determined both the operating room and the patient must be protected from harmful bacteria in order to prevent deadly infections. To ensure a clean surgical treatment, Lister used carbolic acid to sterilize the operating room and surgical instruments. He tested his theory the first time on August 12, 1865, and continued to use it for several years. He then published the incredible results. Surgical mortality had dropped from 45 to 15 percent when using antiseptic practices.[2]

During World War I (1914–1918), French surgeon Alexis Carrel and British chemist Henry Drysdale Dakin used a similar method for treating infected wounds. The Carrel-Dakin treatment is an antiseptic solution containing bleach. When applied to a wound, it speeds up the separation of dead and

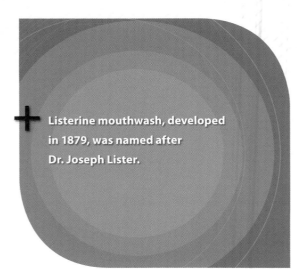

Listerine mouthwash, developed in 1879, was named after Dr. Joseph Lister.

living cells without damaging healthy cells. This was one of many significant contributions Carrel made to the advancement of organ transplant science.

Suturing Blood Vessels & Early Transplants

By the early 1900s, many surgeons were experimenting with organ transplantation, most notably Carrel. As early as 1902, he transplanted a dog's kidney from its abdomen to its neck. But Carrel was only able to do this because he had developed and mastered another technique: suturing blood vessels. Prior to developing his method, patients wounded in a major blood vessel would bleed to death because there was no way to repair the damage. And organ transplants were not possible because there was no way to attach the transplanted organ to its recipient's circulatory system. Carrel experimented with very fine needles and thread until he found the right combination to attach blood vessels from end to end. His basic technique is still used today.

At the same time, Carrel continued his research on organ transplantation. Between 1902 and 1909, Carrel reported successfully transplanting many different organs in animals, including kidneys, thyroid glands, adrenal glands, ovaries, spleens, intestines, and hearts. He also transplanted the thigh of one dog to another, 50 years before the first human limb transplant. In October 1905, Carrel published his first work on organ transplantation, "Functions of a Transplanted Kidney."

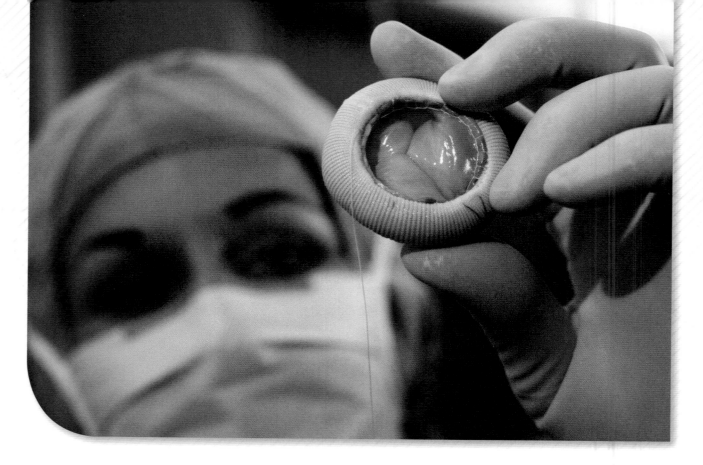

Carrel was not alone in his transplant research. Also in 1905, Austrian ophthalmologist Eduard Zirm restored the sight of an accident victim by performing a human-to-human corneal transplant. Zirm did not recommend the use of corneas from other animal species. Despite this suggestion, most attempted corneal transplants after that were cross species.

Scientists' work on animal transplants eventually led to the use of animal parts, such as pig heart valves, to replace parts in humans.

Animal Experimentation

Scientists have always relied on animals for medical research, and transplant research is no different. Long before Carrel wrote his papers on transplantation, doctors were experimenting with transplant science on animals. In 1749, a physiologist transplanted spurs from a young chicken onto its comb and onto other chickens. These types of experiments continued throughout the 1800s. Giuseppe Boronia grafted the skin of one sheep to the back of another. In England, John Hunter transplanted organs from a male chicken into a female one. And in Ireland, Samuel Bigger transplanted a gazelle cornea into his pet gazelle. Carrel himself tested his suturing methods on cats and dogs, and all of his transplants were performed on animals.

In the early 1900s, doctors also started experimenting with animal-to-human transplants. In 1909, a French surgeon tried to insert slices of rabbit kidney into a child

Another Carrel Contribution

In 1935, Carrel teamed up with famous US aviator Charles Lindbergh to design a perfusion pump. The pump was designed to work outside of the body, and its job was to keep unattached organs, including the heart, alive by circulating blood through them. Although it was not yet practical for surgical purposes, their device was a first step in the development of modern-day heart-lung machines.

suffering from kidney failure. At first the results looked promising, but the child died after two weeks. In 1913, doctors attempted to transplant a monkey kidney into a patient suffering from mercury poisoning, but the girl died shortly after the surgery. This kind of cross species transplantation is called xenotransplantation; it usually fails because the human body rejects the organ.

Researchers were still confident human organ transplantation was possible. In 1933, a research team transplanted the heart of one dog into the neck of another. And in 1953, the first complete heart-lung transplants were performed on dogs. Though these experiments were considered successful, the life expectancy of surviving patients was still counted in days and weeks, not months and years.

In the early 1900s, surgeons also made their first attempts at human-to-human transplants. In 1933, Ukrainian doctor Yu Yu Voronoy performed a human kidney transplant using the kidney of a deceased donor. The recipient's body rejected the new organ and she died. Transplant scientists around the world were beginning to understand that the major remaining roadblock to transplant success was organ rejection.

Sam, a dog with a transplanted heart valve, was just one of many thousands of animals used to test transplantation techniques.

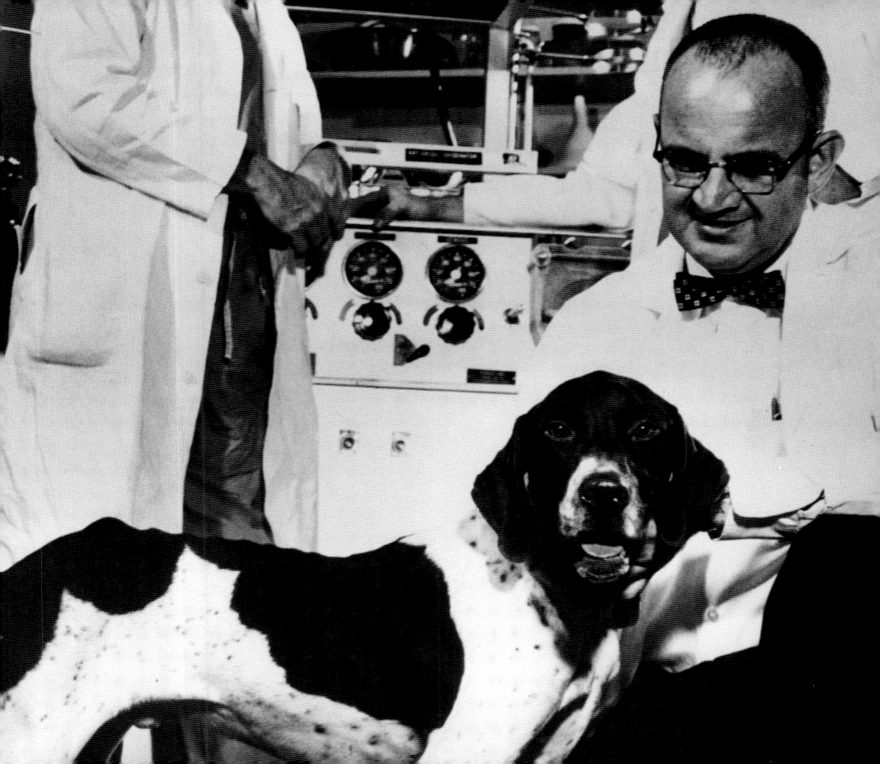

4

Transplant Successes and Failures

By the early 1950s, surgeons had developed the skills and medical knowledge to technically perform transplant surgery, and they were better prepared to operate on human patients. In 1954, Dr. Joseph Murray and a team of surgeons performed the first successful human-to-human kidney transplant at Peter Bent Brigham Hospital in Boston, Massachusetts. Ronald Herrick donated one of his kidneys to his identical twin brother, Richard.

The British immunologist Peter Medawar had already discovered the relationship between donor and recipient made a difference. He treated injured soldiers during World War II (1939–1945). Many of these soldiers required skin grafts, and Medawar noticed rejection rates declined when the donors and recipients were related. The closer the relationship was, the further the rates declined. In the case

Ronald, *left*, and Richard Herrick celebrate the success of their kidney transplant.

A Negative Prediction

When Dr. Murray was offered a job on the transplant team at Peter Bent Brigham Hospital, one of his Harvard professors warned him against accepting the position. "Take that job and you'll ruin your career because there's no chance that transplants will ever work."[1] Dr. Murray went on to prove that professor wrong by performing the first successful kidney transplant.

of identical twins, rejection disappeared entirely. With this information in hand, Murray and his team went to extra lengths to ensure the men were genetically identical. The surgical team tested blood groups and fingerprints. All of the evidence confirmed an identical match. The procedure was a success.

The Decade of Firsts

Many more kidney transplants were successfully performed on identical twins around the world over the next 20 years. The successes taught transplant scientists several things. It was possible to perform a successful organ transplant. A patient's quality of life could be improved with a replacement organ. And the disease that caused the problem in the first place could be cured with an organ transplant.

Moving beyond just twin transplants, surgeons continued to perform organ transplants throughout the

There are many types of transplants. Cross species transplants are called xenografts. Allogeneic transplants are between the same species. Transplants within the same individual—usually skin—are called autografts.

1960s; it was a decade of firsts. In 1963, Dr. Thomas E. Starzl performed the first human liver transplant at the University of Colorado School of Medicine. That same year, Dr. James D. Hardy performed the first lung transplant at the University of Mississippi at Jackson. In 1966, University of Minnesota surgeon Dr. Richard Lillehei performed the first pancreas transplant. The following year, he also performed the first simultaneous kidney and pancreas transplants. Organ transplants were becoming more common, but medical professionals still faced huge obstacles.

Organ Rejection

Transplant surgeons continued to make great strides, but transplant surgeries were still often unsuccessful. Most patients died within days of surgery, either from infection or rejection. Medawar's earlier discoveries about recipient rejection and the donor-recipient relationship helped him determine graft rejection was an immune system response. The immune system fights infections and protects the body from viruses and bacteria by recognizing antigens. It is able to recognize antigens foreign to the body. When it recognizes foreign antigens from transplanted tissues, it attacks them and builds antibodies against them. Rejection occurs when antibodies are directed at a transplanted organ.

Medawar's research also revealed that because an individual's cellular rejection response is defined at an early age, rejection rates can be decreased if foreign cells are introduced before birth or at a very young age. This became known as acquired immunological tolerance. Now that researchers understood why rejection occurred, they knew finding a way to suppress the immune system to prevent organ rejection was pivotal to the future of transplant science.

In the late 1950s and early 1960s, the most common way to suppress the immune system after transplant surgery was with X-ray radiation. But this method weakened the immune system too much; patients would die from

New Hope for Type 1 Diabetes Patients

When Dr. Lillehei performed the first simultaneous kidney and pancreas transplant, he gave new hope to people living with type 1 diabetes, a disease characterized by overly high blood sugar levels. Kidney failure is one common effect of diabetes. Because of this, diabetics did not make good candidates for a kidney transplant. The kidney damage was the result of a faulty pancreas, so the new kidney might also become damaged. By replacing both organs, this problem would be solved. In 2008, more than 800 kidney-pancreas transplants were performed in the United States.[2]

infections because they had no immune system to fight them off. Transplant surgeons knew they had to find a more effective way of suppressing the immune system.

Tissue typing was an important advancement in reducing rejection rates. In the 1950s, Dr. Jean Dausset worked to find out why patients who received multiple blood transfusions had a decreased number of white blood cells. These are the immune system cells that fight disease. During his research, Dausset discovered human leukocyte antigens (HLA). HLAs are molecules located on the surface of white blood cells. They allow the immune system to tell the difference between its own tissues, which it ignores, and foreign tissues, which the body's own disease-fighting antibodies attack. Once Dausset discovered these molecules, he experimented with skin grafts to prove incompatible HLAs resulted in transplant rejection. There are hundreds of variations within six major HLA groups, so finding perfect matches between individuals is nearly impossible. Still, these antigens give good indications of whether or not the tissue of a donor can be successfully transplanted to a recipient, even if a match is imperfect. Today, transplant donors and recipients are tested for both blood and tissue compatibility. The closer the HLA match, the lower the chance of rejection.

Despite the advances made in the field of tissue typing, the early days of organ transplantation were challenging. By 1963, approximately two-thirds of all transplant recipients, not including identical twins, died of organ rejection.[3] Many in the medical field believed the money, time, and energy spent on organ transplant research would be better spent on more promising medical research. Those committed to continuing the organ transplant efforts were often criticized by other medical professionals. But with new immunosuppressive drugs being developed and some success stories emerging, there was reason enough for transplant researchers to continue their work.

Dausset's work in the field of tissue typing broke down a key barrier in the organ transplant procedure.

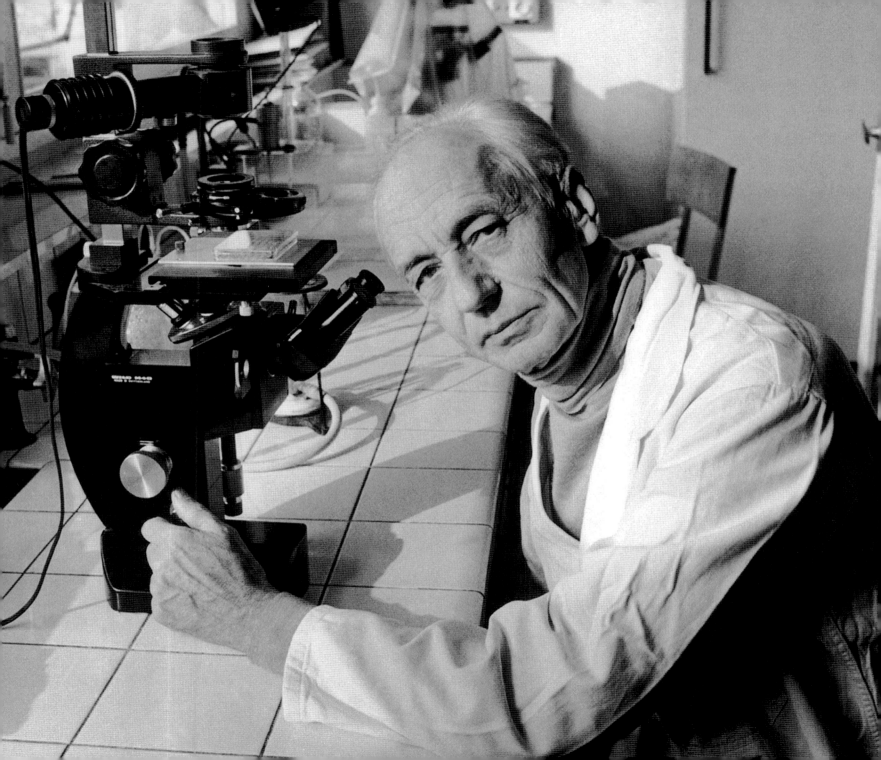

5

The First Human Heart Transplant

By the early 1960s, surgeons around the world had attempted many different types of organ transplant, but no one had performed a human-to-human heart transplant. In 1964, Dr. Hardy attempted to save a dying man by replacing his failing heart with that of a chimpanzee. The surgery was not a success, and other medical professionals at the time criticized the attempt. Several other teams of doctors experimented with heart transplants on dogs. The relative successes of these experiments led them to believe human-to-human heart transplants were not out of reach.

In 1967, four separate surgical research teams were on the verge of being the first to conduct a human-to-human heart transplant. The only thing holding each of them back was the availability of a donor heart. The first doctor to get a compatible heart would win the race.

Christiaan Barnard, *left*, and Adrian Kantrowitz, *right*, talk with surgeon Michael DeBakey, *center*, before appearing on a television talk show in 1967.

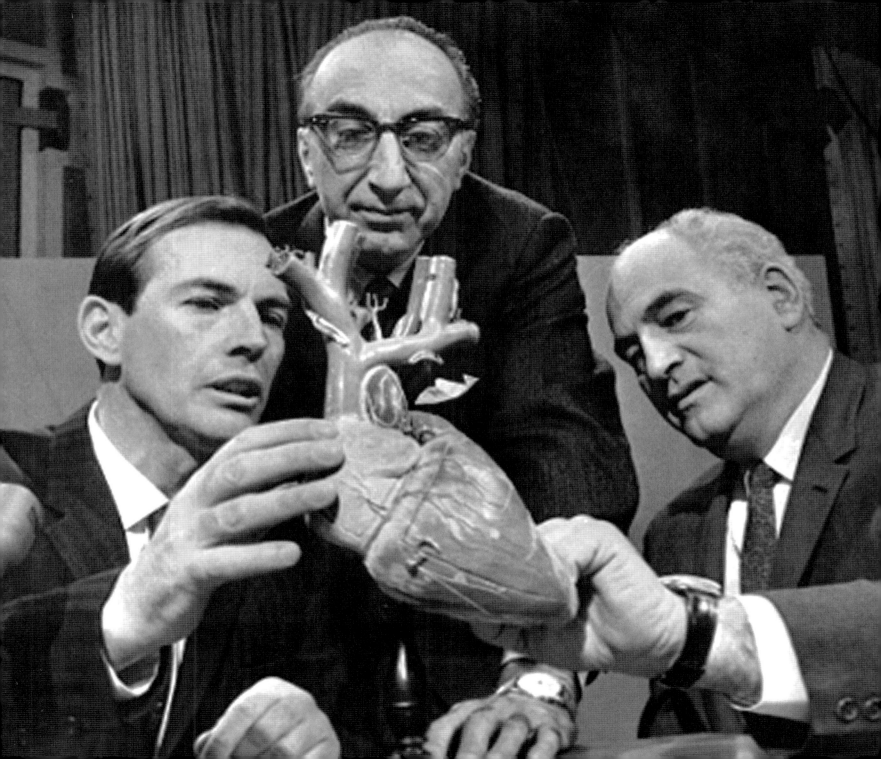

Stopping Blood Flow

In the late 1950s, surgeons Norman Shumway and Richard Lower experimented with topical hypothermia when operating on the heart. They found cooling a localized area of the heart could interrupt blood flow. This would provide a blood-free environment in which to work, making the surgery easier.

The four researchers leading the teams were Dr. Norman Shumway at Stanford University, Dr. Richard Lower at Medical College of Virginia, Dr. Adrian Kantrowitz at Maimonides Hospital in New York, and Dr. Christiaan Barnard at Groote Schuur Hospital in Cape Town, South Africa. Though Barnard worked in South Africa, he had been trained in the United States, visiting major transplant centers and studying the proposed procedure. Each was aware the others were all racing toward the same goal. Lower and Shumway had amassed years of research experience, and Kantrowitz had already come remarkably close to being first.

In June 1966, when a donor heart became available for a baby suffering from terminal congenital heart defects, Kantrowitz was ready to face the challenge. Many of his colleagues, even members of his own surgical team, were uncertain. Still, Kantrowitz believed the only way to advance the research was to move from animal experiments in the lab to human transplants. The donor was a one-day-old baby born with anencephaly. A baby born with anencephaly has a perfectly healthy body, but is missing all or part of its brain, meaning the baby would never have any mental or physical function at all. This condition made the baby an ideal donor, but it also led to major moral and legal dilemmas.

In 1966, US law stated a person was not considered dead until his or her heart stopped beating. Kantrowitz believed his best chance for a successful transplant was if he could take the heart from the donor body while it was still beating. Two members of his surgical team felt he should wait until the heart stopped beating before he began the procedure. He finally agreed to wait, but when he cut into the chest of the donor an hour later, he discovered the heart was too damaged to use. His chance to perform the first heart transplant slipped away.

Barnard's Breakthrough

Almost a year and a half later and on the opposite side of the globe, the opportunity to conduct a human-to-human heart transplant again presented

The parents of the child whose heart was donated in the first attempted heart transplant commented, "We thought we could turn our sorrow into someone else's hope. We're sorry it didn't work out—but we're not sorry we did it."[1]

Dr. Christiaan Barnard

Dr. Christiaan Barnard was born in South Africa in 1922 and began working at Groote Schuur Hospital in Cape Town in 1953. It was here that he had his first big medical achievement, proving fatal gaps in the small intestines of newborn babies are caused by an insufficient blood supply to the fetus during pregnancy. This discovery led to the development of a surgical procedure to correct the defect. Barnard moved to the United States in 1956 to complete his doctoral studies at the University of Minnesota. He returned to Groote Schuur in 1965 as senior cardiothoracic surgeon, where he introduced open-heart surgery to South Africa. Barnard died in 2001.

itself. Like his rivals, Dr. Barnard had been waiting for a donor heart. On December 3, 1967, Myrtle Ann Darvall and her daughter Denise were struck by a car while crossing a road in Cape Town, South Africa. Myrtle Ann was killed instantly. Denise was alive, but her brain was irreparably damaged. Her father gave permission to use her heart in an attempt to save the life of 53-year-old Louis Washkansky, who had been in hospital for three months with a failing heart.

With permission granted, Barnard worked quickly to remove Denise's heart. It is not clear whether he waited for her heart to stop beating before beginning the procedure. In interviews afterward Dr. Barnard said he did wait. But many years later, Dr. Barnard's brother Marius, who assisted him in the surgery, stated the heart was still beating when they removed it from the donor. Either way, the heart was removed and was receiving oxygenated blood from a heart-lung machine within four minutes. The recipient's heart was then removed and replaced by the donor heart. Once the new heart was sutured into place and warmed to body temperature, it started beating. Dr. Barnard had just made history by successfully completing the world's first human-to-human heart transplant.

In the year following Dr. Barnard's successful surgery, 101 more heart transplants were performed around the world, but most patients did not survive more than a few weeks. Despite Medawar's discoveries about immunological response, transplant surgery still remained very risky. Effective immunosuppressive drugs had not yet been developed. Transplant rejection was still more likely than not. In 1969, a clinical moratorium on heart transplant procedures began. This was a collective decision to stop performing the procedure until the issues with the immune system could be resolved. It would be more than a decade before surgeons once again

Heart Transplant Surgery

A heart transplant requires two surgical teams: one to remove the organ from the donor and a second to transplant the organ into the recipient. As soon as a donor heart becomes available, it is removed and stored in a special solution to keep it cool and preserve it through transportation. In the meantime, the recipient's medical team is notified a heart is on its way so they can prepare the patient. The patient is put under an anesthetic and hooked up to a heart machine to keep him or her alive while the heart is being removed. The machine allows blood to continue to flow throughout the body while bypassing the heart. The patient's heart is then cooled and cut out. The new heart is sewn into place and blood vessels are attached. When the new heart warms up again, blood begins to pump through it.

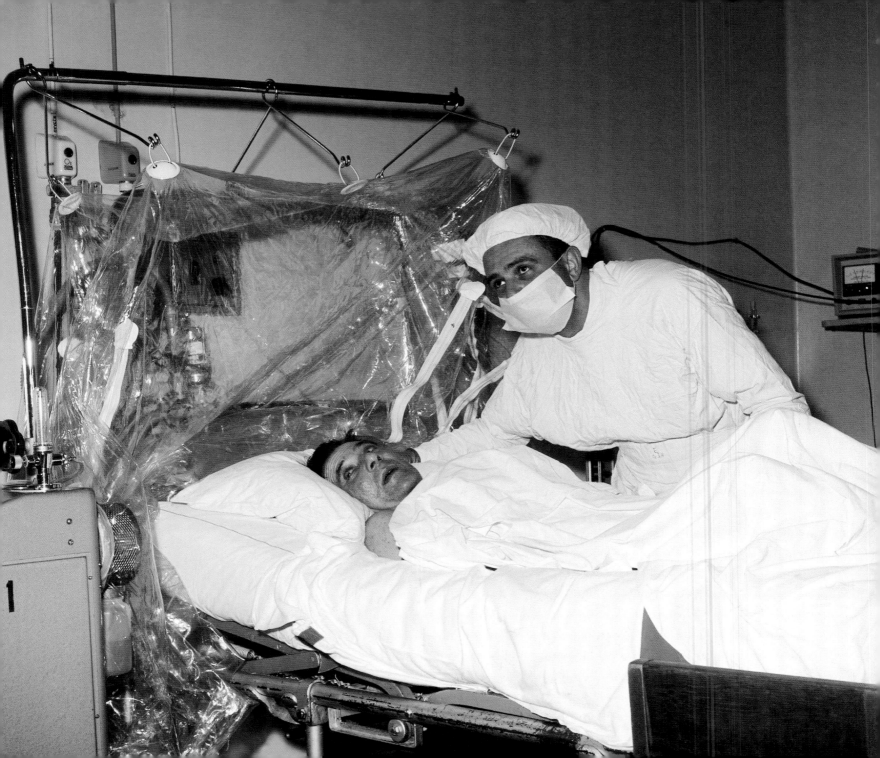

started performing human heart transplants on a regular basis.

Dr. Norman Shumway conducted the first adult human-to-human heart transplant in the United States at Stanford University on January 6, 1968.

Dr. Barnard, *right*, with heart transplant recipient Louis Washkansky after the historic surgery

6

Organg Donations

Organ transplants would not be possible without organ donors and the network of systems that brings donors and recipients together. Moral, ethical, and legal debates about organ supply have been an issue since the idea of transplanting human organs first arose. On top of this are complex logistical issues: tracking eligible recipients, matching recipients and donors, and finally arranging safe and fast transport of the organs. Many people must do hard work behind the scenes to make sure donated organs make it to desperately waiting recipients. It is a big job, and it is not easy.

Organ donors in many countries carry cards to indicate their willingness to donate organs after death.

Donor Card
I would like to help someone to live after my death.
Let your relatives know your wishes, and keep this card with you at all times.

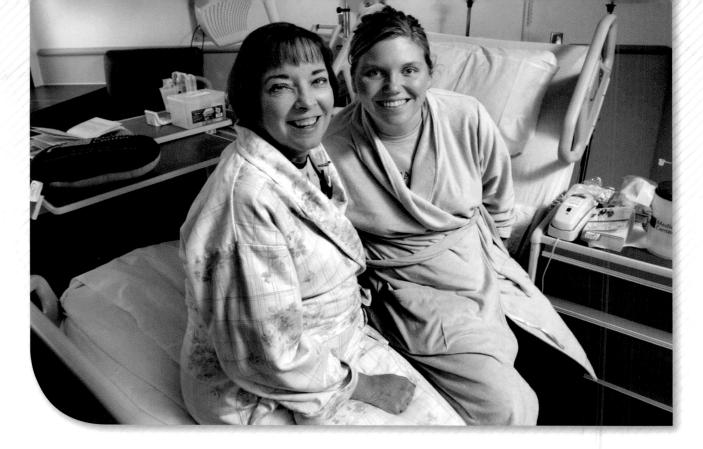

Organ Donors

There are two types of organ donors: living and deceased. Living donors can donate a kidney, the lobe of a lung, or part of the liver or pancreas. Like the Herrick brothers, most living donors are family members. However, there are other types of living donors. Nonrelated donors are people emotionally close but not related by blood to transplant candidates. Anonymous donors, on the other hand, are

A kidney recipient, *left*, poses with her living donor. More than 5,000 living US donors gave their kidneys in 2012.

not known by the recipient and make their donation for selfless reasons. Paired donation is when two sets of kidney donors and recipients swap donors to receive a kidney from a compatible blood type. Some areas of the country also offer a kidney donor waiting list exchange, where a donor who is not compatible with an intended recipient can donate to a stranger in exchange for the intended recipient being moved ahead on the waiting list for a deceased donor.

Living donors go through a rigorous screening process to ensure they are both physically and emotionally able to handle surgery and recovery. Once they pass this screening process, the risks to donors are relatively low. It is possible in any surgery for complications to arise, but studies have shown donors' life expectancies do not change. The human body is a remarkable machine that can adapt. After donating a kidney, the remaining kidney grows larger to compensate for the lost one. The liver can regenerate and regain full function after a section is removed. Although the lungs and pancreas do not regenerate, donors are able to live on with no noticeable impact on their health due to reduced function. Donor recovery time from surgery is relatively quick, with most donors back to their usual routine two to six weeks after the procedure.

The other type of organ donor is deceased. These are people who, prior to death, indicate their desire to donate by adding themselves to a state registry of organ donors. They can do this simply by noting it on their driver's license, giving paramedics and doctors a quick indication of their preference.

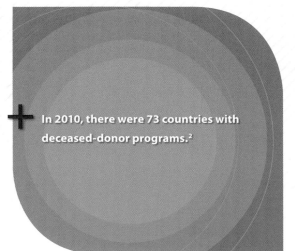

In 2010, there were 73 countries with deceased-donor programs.[2]

People usually tell their family members they wish to donate as well, so the family can support this decision after death. Those in need of heart, double-lung, or cornea transplants have to rely on deceased donors. In 2011, there were more than 14,000 organ donors—8,127 deceased and 6,017 living—resulting in 28,535 transplants.[1] When a donor dies, multiple organs can be harvested, resulting in many more transplants than donors. Deceased donations are not always voluntary. In some states, corneas may be harvested without the consent or knowledge of the deceased person's family.

Organ Allocation

The National Organ Transplant Act of 1984 called for a unified transplant network to be operated by a private nonprofit organization. The Organ Procurement and Transplantation Network (OPTN) was formed, and in 1986 the US Department of Health and Human Services awarded the United Network for Organ Sharing (UNOS) the contract to operate the OPTN. The OPTN is responsible for the organ matching and placement process; it keeps a fully staffed organ center operational 24 hours a day. It also develops policies and procedures for organ recovery, collection, and transportation. Finally, it collects and manages data about organ donation and transplantation. The OPTN uses a secure Web-based computer system to maintain the nation's organ transplant waiting list and keep track of the recipient and donor organ characteristics.

Hospitals are required to notify their local organ procurement organization (OPO) of every patient who has died or is near dying. The hospital provides the OPO with information about the deceased to determine whether he or she is a potential donor. If the patient is a potential donor candidate, an OPO representative goes to the hospital. The OPO representative is responsible for finding out if the patient is registered as a donor in the state. If the donor is not registered, the representative then seeks permission from the family. If consent is given,

+ The Organ Gap

The gap between the number of people waiting for an organ and organ donations increases every year. In the United States in 1989, there were 5,927 donors and 17,917 people on the transplant waiting list. By 2009, there were 14,630 donors and 105,567 people on the waiting list.[3]

By the Numbers

Number of people waiting for an organ transplant in 2013	117,677
Number of people who die each day waiting for an organ transplant	18
Number of lives one donor can save	8
Number of people who receive an organ transplant each day	79
Number of people registered to be a donor in the United States	100 million [4]
Number of donors in 2011	14,144
Number of organ transplants in 2011	28,535
Number of cornea transplants in 2011	46,000
Number of tissue transplants in 2011	1 million [5]

a complete medical evaluation is done on the deceased person, including both a medical and a social history. If everything passes the screening, the search for a matching recipient begins.

The OPTN keeps a database of all patients in the United States waiting for a transplant. A computer program matches donor organs with recipients based on blood and tissue types, height, weight, and age. How long the patient has been waiting, the severity of illness, and the distance between the donor's and the recipient's hospitals are also factored in when determining who is the best match for a specific organ. The program does not reference or make matches based on race, gender, income, or social status. A list of patients who match the donor is generated, and each organ is offered to the first patient on the computer match list. The transplant surgeon may accept or decline the organ. Reasons for declining the organ include a patient who is too sick for surgery or a patient who cannot be reached in time. Approximately 75 percent of available organs go to local patients; the remaining 25 percent are shared with patients in other parts of the country.[6]

Preservation and Transportation

While the search for matching recipients is taking place, doctors are maintaining the donor's life through artificial support while monitoring each of the organs. Once organs and recipients have been matched, the OPO representative coordinates the arrival and departure times of the transplant surgical teams.

Once in the operating room, surgeons carefully remove organs, followed by tissue such as bones, corneas, and skin. Organs remain healthy for a very short period of time after removal and must be carefully stored for transportation. Each organ needs to be stored differently. Livers are transported in a

Federal law outlines detailed procedures for packing organs for transport. For example, kidneys and pancreases must be placed in a rigid container, but hearts, livers, and lungs do not require a rigid container.

HUMAN ORGAN
FOR TRANSPLANT
PLEASE HANDLE WITH CARE!

Recipientcenter (Empfängerzentrum)

ET-No. (ET-Nr.)
D-No. (D-Nr.)
Transport ☐Car (Auto) ☐Plane (Flugzeug) ☐Train (Zug)
Airport/Station (Zielflughafen/-bahnhof)
Transfer station (Zwischenstation)
Flight-/Train-No. (Flugzeug-/Zug-Nr.)

Despatched by (Absender)

DSO.
DEUTSCHE STIFTUNG
ORGANTRANSPLANTATION
Gemeinnützige Stiftung

Organisationszentrale Berlin
Straße des 17. Juni 106 - 106
10623 Berlin
Germany

Tel. +49 800 488 00 88
Fax +49 69 677328 2088

Koordinierungsstelle Organspende

☐ Kidney (Niere)
☐ Liver (Leber)
☐ Pancreas (Pankreas)
☐ Heart (Herz)
☐ Lung (Lunge)

Report inside!

cooled saltwater solution that preserves the organ for up to eight hours. There are two methods for storing and transporting kidneys: machine perfusion, which pumps a preservation solution through the kidney during transportation, or cold static storage, where the kidney is filled with a sterile preservation fluid and is kept on ice in a box. The most common method of storing hearts for transportation is in a camping cooler on ice. In all cases, the organs must be transplanted into the recipient as quickly as possible. In addition to ambulances, airplanes and helicopters are often contracted to get the organs and medical teams where they need to be. But none of this could take place without people donating in the first place.

Beating Heart in a Box

Organs do not survive long once removed from the human body. Medical teams race as fast as they can after removing the organ to put it on ice and get it to the waiting recipient, and every second counts. In 2011, a company called TransMedics began running clinical trials on the Organ Care System (OCS). The OCS is an organ preservation system that keeps a donor heart functioning outside of the body after it has been removed from the donor. The device keeps the heart warm and beating with oxygen-rich and nutrient-rich blood while in transport. The company hopes to prove the heart can survive longer and sustain less damage when using the OCS.

Organs must be transported and stored quickly and carefully to ensure the tissue does not become damaged.

Improving Survival Rates

In response to the high failure rate of transplant surgery through the late 1960s and 1970s, several groups of researchers continued to look for ways to solve the problem of organ rejection. During this period, many important discoveries were made that finally increased the success rate of transplant surgery. The procedure was eventually turned into a legitimate medical option that gave dying patients hope.

New Drugs, New Beginning

Transplant scientists were well aware organ rejection was the major obstacle standing in the way of true transplant success. As early as 1960, William Dameshek realized if formation of antibodies could be prevented in transplant recipients, the tissue graft would survive for a longer time. He also

Joseph Murray won a Nobel Prize in 1990 for his work on the largest problem in organ transplants: rejection of the new organ.

Professional Transplant Organizations

The American Society of Transplant Surgeons consists of almost 2,000 surgeons, scientists, and other health professionals. It was founded in 1974 with the aim of uniting surgeons involved in the field of transplantation. Founded in 1982, the American Society of Transplantation is an organization of more than 3,000 transplant professionals. The professionals come from all transplant fields, including research, surgery, education, and patient care. The goal of the organization is to offer a "forum for the exchange of knowledge, scientific information, and expertise in the field of transplantation."[1]

determined that a drug called 6-MP worked to block this immune response. Scientist Roy Calne started experimenting with 6-MP when performing kidney transplants on dogs. Some dogs lived for months. This proved to scientists for the first time that rejection could be prevented with the use of a chemical immunosuppressive, a drug that prevents the immune system from carrying out its normal response to foreign tissue. Calne then started experimenting on dogs with azathioprine—a drug related to 6-MP—and achieved even better results.

In 1962, Dr. Murray at Brigham Hospital in Boston was the first doctor to use azathioprine on a human kidney transplant recipient. The patient survived 17 months, once again giving researchers hope. However, subsequent transplant recipients did not do as well with the drug, and enthusiasm started to fade. Dr. Starzl then decided to try administering azathioprine to organ recipients before the transplant surgery. He also administered a steroid called prednisone. The results were excellent; one of Starzl's kidney transplant patients was still alive 50 years later.

Encouraged by these results, Starzl started attempting liver transplants. His first in 1963 was a failure. Later patients survived for several weeks, confirming transplanted livers could work. However, surgeons worldwide decided to stop performing liver transplants until they could figure out why patients were not surviving longer. Through their research they discovered none of the transplanted organs showed signs of rejection. Instead, bacterial infections had killed the patients. Researchers needed to find the right dose of immunosuppressant medications to give patients. Too little would not protect the organ from rejection, but too much would leave the patient unable to fight off ordinary bacterial infections. It was four years before Starzl reopened his transplant program and performed his next

+ Longest Living Kidney Transplant Recipient

In January 1963, Bob Phillips received a new kidney donated by his sister. The siblings were not a good match—they were not even the same blood type. But Starzl took a chance, counting on the new immunosuppressive drugs. Three weeks after the surgery, Phillips's new kidney started to fail. He began to retain liquid and put on weight. Both doctors and patient were discouraged. Then one night, his kidney suddenly started to function. The kidney never failed again. In 2012, the 86-year-old Phillips went for his annual kidney test. Nearly 50 years later, it was still functioning perfectly.

liver transplant using a new combination of drugs. Success rates improved, and in 1968, Calne opened the country's second liver transplant program.

Calne and Starzl both continued their research into immunosuppressive drugs. In 1980, Calne introduced cyclosporine as an option. Cyclosporine is a very potent drug; though it was effective at suppressing the immune response, it also could do severe damage to the kidneys. Starzl combined cyclosporine with prednisone to help reduce this negative impact on the kidneys, and liver transplant patients began surviving for more than a year after surgery. In 1983, the US surgeon general concluded liver transplants had finally passed beyond experimental status and could be administered regularly. Cyclosporine transformed the success of organ transplantation and is still the most commonly used antirejection drug today.

New Technologies

While antirejection drugs improved, so too did medical technology. Surgeons had proven organ transplantation was a viable medical option for patients suffering from end-stage organ disease.

The world's longest-living liver-transplant patient is Kim Hudson. Starzl replaced her failing liver in 1970; she was still thriving in 2012.

Heart transplant recipient Paul Posharow must take approximately 30 pills every day for the rest of his life following his surgery.

SUN MORN
MON MORN
TUE MORN
WED MORN
THU MORN
FRI MORN
SAT MORN
SUN NOON
MON NOON
TUE NOON
WED NOON
THU NOON
FRI NOON
SAT NOON
SUN BED
MON BED
TUE BED
WED BED
THU BED
FRI BED
SAT BED
SUN EVE
MON EVE
TUE EVE
WED EVE
THU EVE
FRI EVE
SAT EVE

A shortage of organs, however, was always a challenge, and patients often died waiting for an organ. From the beginning of organ transplant research, there have always been more people in need of new organs than there are organs available. The development of man-made alternatives has gone a long way to extend patients' lives and improve transplant survival rates.

Dr. Kantrowitz in particular made many significant contributions, inventing more than 20 mechanical devices to improve the lives of patients, including those needing heart transplants. Although he performed the first human heart transplant in the United States, Kantrowitz concentrated his work on finding ways to artificially support the natural heart with the circulatory devices he invented. One of his inventions, the LVAD, allowed heart patients to leave the hospital and live relatively normal lives while waiting for a heart to become available.

The extra time the LVAD gave patients was important, but many still died while waiting for an organ. Doctors worked to invent mechanical hearts. In 1969, Denton Cooley implanted the first mechanical heart in a human patient, who survived for 60 hours. It was not until 1982, however, that the first permanent mechanical heart was introduced. Robert Jarvik developed the Jarvik-7, a permanent artificial heart with an internal power system. The power system regulated a pump through a network of compressed air hoses that entered the heart through the chest. The air hoses were connected to the heart chambers. Jarvik tested the device on animals to ensure the heart could consistently beat at least

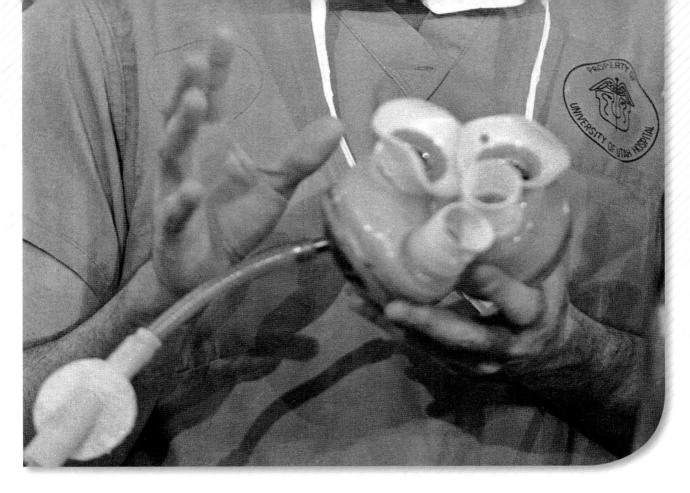

100,000 times a day before it was tested on a human.[2] When it was finally implanted in a human, the first patient lived 112 days before dying of multiple organ failure. Several more Jarvik-7s were implanted, with one patient surviving 18 months with the device. Now doctors knew they had more time to find patients an organ donor.

Risks, Rewards, & Failures

With transplant success rates improving, the number of organ transplants began increasing. There were more firsts, and surgeons also took more risks. In 1984, doctors performed the first successful heart transplant on a child. The four-year-old boy needed a second transplant in 1989, but he was alive and well in 2013. It was also in 1984 that doctors in Loma Linda, California, implanted the heart of a baboon into a 12-day-old girl. The baby survived 20 days before rejecting the organ. The procedure was extremely controversial.

Between 1984 and 1999, doctors performed many xenotransplantations with little success. In 1992, Polish surgeons tried to implant the heart of a pig into a human patient, but the patient survived less than 24 hours. Dr. Starzl tried transplanting a baboon liver into a patient in 1992, but immunosuppressive drugs weakened the patient's system to the point where he was unable to fight off an infection. The patient died soon after. These failures and many more led to the US Food and Drug Administration (FDA) banning the use of nonhuman

"If ever there was a field that developed against the grain, that was costly to people who worked in it, whose engagement meant that for most of their career they would work for substandard income compared with their peers. . . . it would be transplantation."[3]

—Dr. Thomas Starzl

primates in transplantations in 1999. And in 2000, the International Society for Heart and Lung Transplantation advised clinical xenotransplantations should be stopped until a minimum virus risk was determined. They did, however, agree "xenotransplantation has the potential to solve the problem of donor organ supply, and therefore research in this field should be actively encouraged and supported."[4]

Controversy and Challenges

Although organ transplants have become relatively common, controversy and challenges still surround them. Animal rights groups protest both animal experimentation and xenotransplantation. A shortage of organs has led to debates about donor family compensation and the buying and selling of body parts, as well as the emergence of an underground illegal market for human organs. And defining death and the proper time to remove organs from a donor is an ever-evolving issue. For transplant researchers, surgeons, and patients, the benefits of organ transplants outweigh the controversies and challenges associated with them. Still, debates rage on.

One challenge that exists in nearly all transplant surgeries is the change in lifestyle for patients after the procedure. Once organs have been transplanted, patients' struggles are far from over.

Indian activists protest against a major illegal kidney sales program uncovered in 2008.

KIDNEY RACKET
WE DEMAND
CBI ENQUIRY

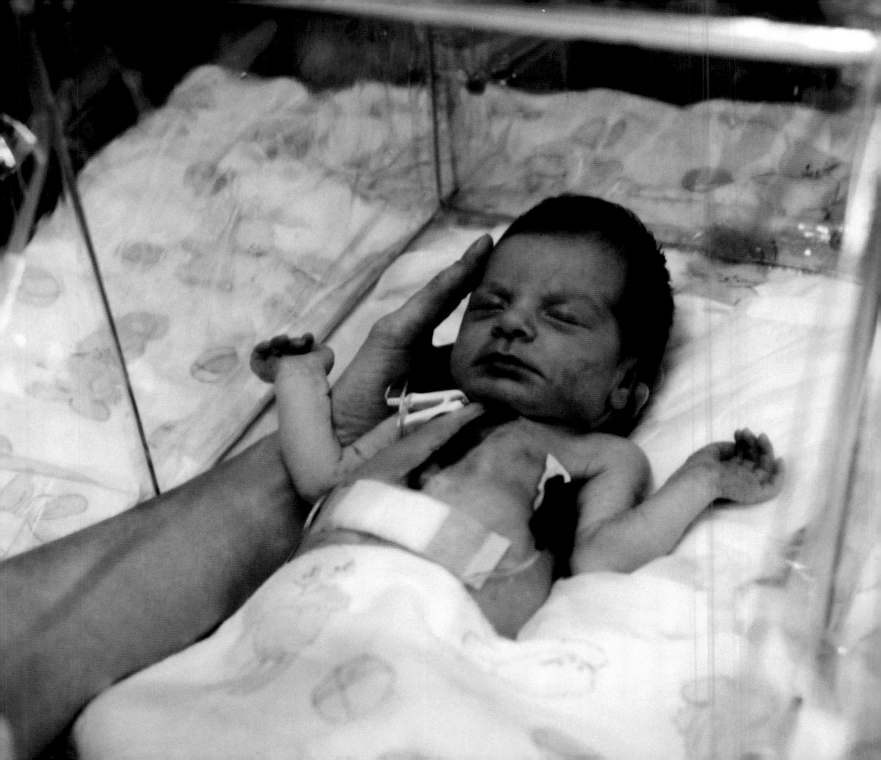

They must continue to take immunosuppressive drugs for their entire lives. Many patients struggle with emotional issues and depression, knowing that another person's life had to end in order for theirs to continue. Support groups exist to help organ recipients cope with the aftereffects of an organ transplant.

Animal to Human Transplants

Although human organ transplants never would have taken place if not for the experimental research done on animals, many believe humans have no right to use animals in this way. One of the most vocal opponents of xenotransplantation is People for the Ethical Treatment of Animals (PETA). The organization refers to xenotransplantation as "Frankenstein science."[1] In 1999, it formally asked the FDA to ban all xenotransplantation experiments.

But those who are in favor of the science argue it is impossible to support cancer, AIDS, and diabetes research while at the same time opposing animal research. For this reason, some have accepted animal experimentation is the only way to advance medical research. The idea of replacing human organs with animal ones still worries others.

One of the strongest medical arguments against this kind of surgery is cross contamination. Opponents are concerned animal organs can transfer deadly animal viruses to humans—not just to

The 1984 xenotransplantation of a baboon heart into a baby was condemned for both scientific and ethical reasons.

the organ recipient, but also to health-care workers and family members. For example, pigs carry a virus called porcine endogenous retrovirus, which British scientists believed could infect human cells in a laboratory. In 2004, scientists at Harvard Medical School tested this theory, transplanting both pig and human cells into mice. After six months, the human cells were not infected. But this did little to alleviate fears.

Organ transplants from other primates, such as chimpanzees and baboons, to humans have been ruled out. Despite supporting xenotransplantation research, the US National Academy of Sciences (NAS) and the United Kingdom's Nuffield Council on Bioethics both oppose the use of primates for xenotransplantation because of their likeness to humans. As noted by a professor at the University of Texas Medical Branch, "It's not going to happen, [with] the worries that we rightly have over infectious disease from primates. . . and also because we could decimate the entire primate population and we still wouldn't have enough organs."[2]

Pigs are the animal most xenotransplantation research is focused on. As the NAS explains, "these animals are traditionally used as a source of food, are distant from humans phylogenetically, and fall much lower on the personhood scale."[3] PETA disagrees, but the Humane Society of the United States has cautiously supported animal experimentation, stating that "biomedical research has advanced the

The Value of Human Organs

Human body parts can be worth a lot of money. The value of a human heart has been estimated at $119,000. One estimate gauges the following prices for other major organs:

Skin	$10 per square inch
Liver	$157,000
Kidney	$262,000
Spleen	$508
Gallbladder	$1,219
Small Intestine	$2,519 [6]

health of both people and animals. . . and the research community is concerned about the welfare of the animals they use."[4]

Organs for Dollars

The ever-growing shortage of organs has led to a sinister problem: the illegal sale of human organs. Selling human organs is illegal in almost every country in the world, Iran being a notable exception. In the United States, the National Organ Transplant Act of 1984 imposed criminal penalties of up to $50,000 and five years in prison on any person who "knowingly acquire[s], receive[s], or otherwise transfer[s] any human organ for valuable consideration for use in human transplantation."[5] The primary concerns surrounding donor compensation are that sellers might be exploited, buyers could be victimized, and that it would be too difficult to design and regulate an effective market system.

However, people will go to extreme measures when faced with death. The World Health Organization reported more than 10,000 black market operations involving illegally purchased organs took place in 2012—more than one every hour.[7] Those seeking organs travel to places such as China, Pakistan, or India. The organs—usually kidneys—are sometimes harvested from poor and desperate people who are compensated only a few thousand dollars. This puts both the donor and the recipient at tremendous medical risk. A Michigan State University anthropologist published an in-depth study of the black market for human kidneys. He interviewed 33 kidney sellers in Bangladesh and found they usually did not receive the promised compensation. The sellers also suffered severe health issues as a result of the surgery. In many cases the recipient did not survive either.

This black market is why some people support the idea of creating a legal compensation system for human organ donation, arguing it is the illegality of the commercial trade of organs that creates the underground market. People have shown some degree of acceptance to this idea. In 2004, the Organ Donation and Recovery Improvement Act allowed authorities to provide reimbursement of travel and subsistence expenses for living organ donors. And a 2012 survey from Canada reported 45 percent of respondents think it is acceptable to offer money as an incentive to living donors. Some 70 percent of respondents said cash payment is an acceptable way to entice people to donate their organs after death.[8]

Brain Death

Determining what defines death is one of the most controversial of all transplant issues. When it is defined as the absence of a heartbeat, doctors are required to wait for a patient's heart to stop beating before they could remove organs for transplant recipients. Damage to organs occurs very quickly after death, and if they are too damaged they are unsuitable for donation. For this reason, the organs of brain-dead donors can be collected more easily. Although the person is irreversibly dead, most of the body continues functioning, keeping the organs healthy for transplantation.

In 1968, Dr. Lower pushed legal boundaries when he removed the heart of a man he determined brain-dead but whose heart was still beating. The dead man's family was

A Kidney for an iPad

Organ brokers sometimes find their donors through newspaper ads. The brokers make outrageous promises in exchange for a kidney. In 2012, when researching the human organ black market, a British newspaper contacted an organ broker in China. The broker was advertising his services with the slogan "Donate a kidney, buy the new iPad." He was offering just under $4,000 for the organ and said the operation would take place in ten days. [9]

not notified. Lower then transplanted the heart into a waiting recipient. The family of the dead man sued Lower in a million-dollar wrongful death suit. Although the jury ultimately concluded no wrongful death occurred, the case stirred the debate about what determined death and when it is appropriate to remove organs from a donor.

It would be almost a decade before the National Conference of Commissioners on Uniform State Laws drafted the Uniform Determination of Death Act (UDDA). The UDDA states, "An individual who has sustained either irreversible cessation of circulatory and respiratory functions, or irreversible cessation of all function of the entire brain, including the brain stem, is dead. A determination of death must be made in accordance with accepted medical standards."[10] It was endorsed by the American Bar and Medical Associations and adopted by 45 states.

The UDDA meant a brain-dead person who is warm with a beating heart and ventilating lungs is legally just as dead as a person whose heart has permanently stopped beating and whose body has turned cold. Applying these definitions of death,

Brain death is caused by an insufficient supply of oxygen to the brain, causing the brain cells to die.

surgeons have followed the ethics of the dead donor rule (DDR). Under this rule, it is considered wrong to end one person's life to save another. The DDR is meant to assure patients, families, and health professionals that patients determined brain-dead are truly dead.

However, in 2011, the UNOS put forward recommendations to update and clarify language surrounding donation after cardiac death (DCD) that somewhat confuses the DDR. Each year, more transplant surgeons are removing organs from donors who have suffered severe brain injury but are not technically brain-dead. This can occur if a patient or family, before death, requests life support be stopped. After the patient is removed from life support, the heart takes anywhere from a few minutes to an hour to stop beating. The usual procedure has been for surgeons to wait anywhere from two to five minutes after the heart stops beating before they pronounce the patient dead and begin to remove organs.

Controversy arises from the fact that the UDDA states irreversible cessation of circulatory and respiratory functions must exist before death is declared. But cardiopulmonary resuscitation (CPR) can often restore a heartbeat after it has stopped beating for 15 minutes or longer, meaning it may be possible to revive a person some surgeons might consider dead. Bioethicists are concerned about the UNOS's recommendations because they do not specify a waiting time, essentially allowing individual hospitals to develop their own definition of death. Many find this idea disturbing. On the other hand,

Resistance to Transplantation in Japan

Some objections to organ transplants are cultural. This is the case for some Japanese people who follow traditional views based on the religion of Shintoism. Those who follow Shintoism believe the soul rests in the human body. They also believe the soul is polluted by death for 49 days and is therefore not fully dead. These beliefs make it difficult for many Japanese people to accept brain death. It was not until 1997 that the Japanese government passed a law allowing for death pronouncement based on the brain. However, brain death can only be pronounced in cases where organs are being donated, and then only if the deceased person previously agreed to organ donation and the brain-based criteria for death. His or her family must also agree.

the UNOS claims the change will increase the number of organs procured from DCD, increasing the number of transplants and ultimately the number of lives saved.

Transplant surgeon Juro Wada was investigated for murder when officials discovered he had failed to prove whether a patient was brain-dead.

9

Transplants Today and Tomorrow

Organ transplant science has been developing at a rapid pace since the 1980s. Both lab and clinical research have opened the doors to a whole new era of transplant surgery. From improved surgical procedures and techniques to mechanical parts, engineered tissue, and bioartificial organs, every part of the science is moving toward ever more remarkable procedures.

Organ transplant success rates continue to rise. Sterile operating procedures and state-of-the-art equipment, combined with advanced tissue matching and antirejection drugs, have resulted in 91 percent of kidney transplant patients now surviving three years after surgery.[1] A 2008 Canadian study showed lung transplant survival rates also continue to improve, noting that three-year survival rates increased from 60 percent in 1997 to 80 percent in 2003.[2] The same is true for heart transplant

Some modern artificial hearts are worn outside the body rather than being fully implanted.

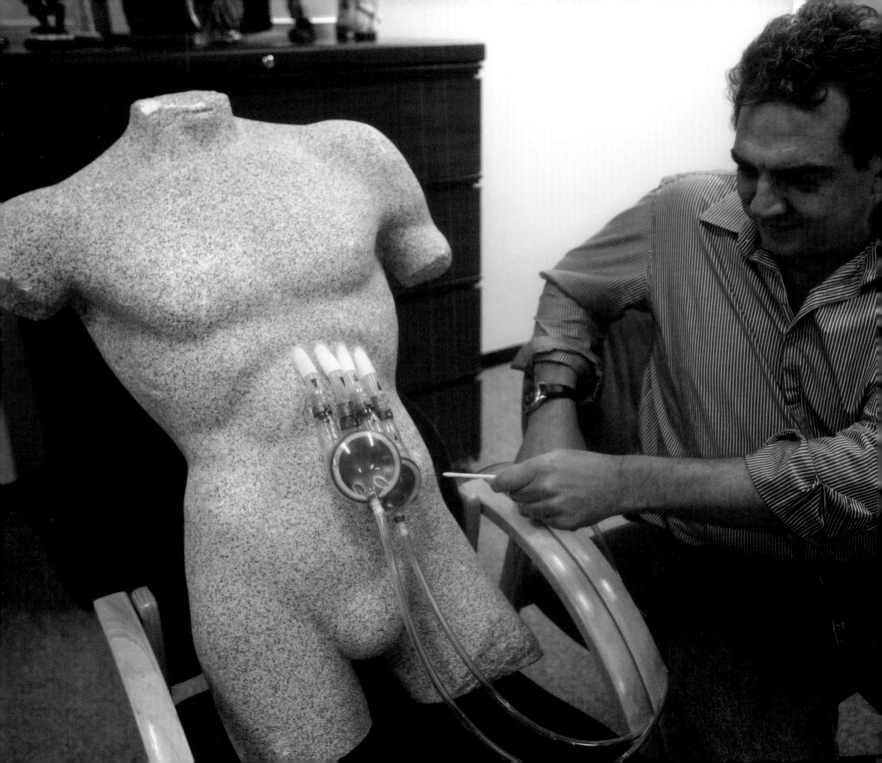

patients, with 75 percent of patients surviving five years.[3]

Transplant Trailblazer Amazed by Progress

In a 2004 *New York Times* article, Starzl spoke about the rapid growth of transplantation:

The growth of transplantation from ground zero to its present state seems like a fairy tale, a fantasy that became reality because of the courage of our patients. The truth is that none of us in the 1950s remotely envisioned the height to which transplantation would rise and the way it has changed the face of medicine.[4]

Face Transplants

In 2005, doctors at Amiens University Hospital in northern France spent 15 hours performing the world's first face transplant. The recipient, Isabelle Dinoire, received a new nose, lips, and a chin. For people who have suffered facial disfigurement in accidents, facial transplant surgery can have a profound impact on their lives. In particular, the injuries suffered by soldiers have spurred more research and development in this area of transplant surgery.

In 2012, a surgical team at the University of Maryland Medical Center performed the most complex face transplant to date. Patient Richard Lee Norris lost most of his lips, nose, and jaws in a 1997 gun accident. For 15 years he lived as a recluse, hiding behind a surgical mask. The 2012

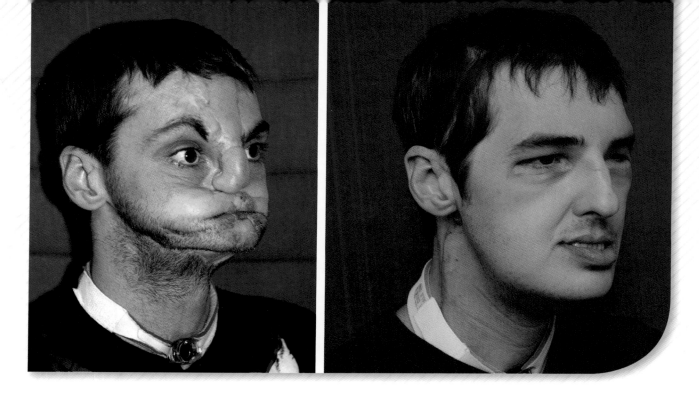

surgery replaced his jaws, teeth, tongue, skin, and underlying nerve and muscle tissue from his scalp to neck. Seven months after surgery, doctors reported he was doing remarkably well. Norris himself said, "I am now able to walk past people and no one even gives me a second look. . . . I am doing well. I spend a lot of my time fishing and working on my golf game. I am also enjoying time with my family and friends."[5]

Organ Transplant Chain

History was made in 2011 when 60 different people participated in the longest chain of organ transplants to date. It all started in California when a man donated his kidney to an anonymous recipient. The niece of that recipient, who was a willing donor but was not a match for her aunt, offered to donate a kidney to someone else on the transplant waiting list. This gesture created a domino effect that ultimately involved coordination between 17 hospitals in 11 states over a period of four months. By the end, 30 Americans had received kidney transplants.[6]

Growing Human Organs

When everything goes right, organ transplant surgery can seem miraculous. However, the ongoing shortage of donor organs, combined with the growing number of people on organ waiting lists, continues to stand in the way of many lifesaving surgeries. Researchers have developed a number of external and internal devices that can prolong the lives of people with failing organs. Mechanical hearts have vastly improved and can be transplanted to do the work of a human heart. Diabetics can wear an artificial pancreas that monitors and controls their blood sugar levels. And scientists are working to develop a miniature dialysis machine that can be transplanted into patients with kidney failure. But these are all mechanical solutions that fall short of the real thing. The future of transplant surgery appears to be in tissue engineering and bioartificial organs.

Liver cells grown in a petri dish can already be used to clean the blood of patients with liver diseases.

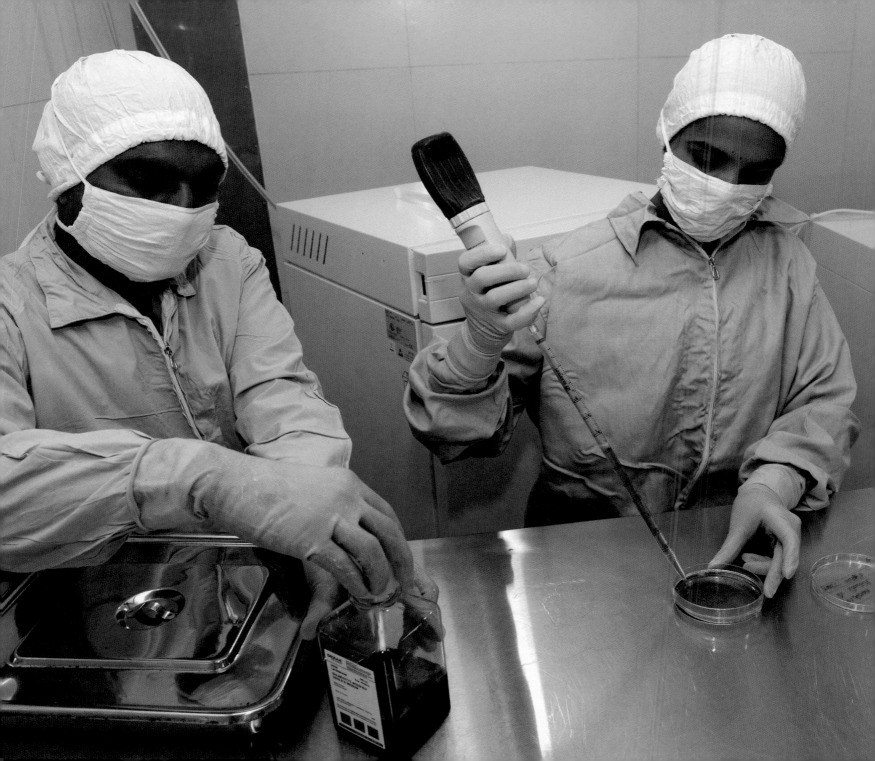

Tissue engineering involves the fields of applied biology and biomedical engineering. Researchers in these fields are studying ways to create artificial organs for transplantation. Applying the body's own ability to regenerate, researchers are working on ways to grow new organs from patients' own stem cells. Stem cells are cells found in the human body that have the potential to develop into any cell type. There are many benefits to learning how to grow these cells into new organs. For one thing, it would solve the organ shortage problem. Also, organ rejection would no longer be a problem. Since the tissue would be grown from the patient's own cells, immunosuppressive drugs would not be necessary.

Scientists are achieving amazing things with tissue engineering, particularly with respect to bioartificial organs. Labs around the world have started to experiment with scaffolds, the parts left over when organs are stripped of most of their cells. Scaffolds are compounds that act like brick mortar to hold cells in their proper place. One goal is to use these stripped natural scaffolds to build new organs by reseeding them with the transplant recipients' cells. The creation of complex organs such as livers and kidneys is still a long way off, but most who work in the field believe they are within reach.

Researchers have had some success with simpler organs. More than 30 people have received lab-grown bladders. Because bladders are relatively simple hollow organs with fewer blood vessels than solid organs like the heart or liver, they are less complex and easier to grow artificially. Scientists remove healthy cells from a patient's diseased bladder and multiply them in a laboratory. When they have

Stem cell researchers may be at the frontier of the next breakthroughs in the field of organ transplants.

reproduced enough healthy cells, they apply the cells to a balloon-shaped scaffold. Different cells need to be applied to different parts of the scaffold. Muscle cells go on the outside and cells lining the urinary tract go on the inside. The new bladder is then incubated for up to eight weeks until the cells form functioning tissue. Finally, it is transplanted into the patient.

In 2011, Dr. Paolo Macchiarini at the Karolinska Institute in Sweden implanted a new windpipe into a man whose own windpipe had a cancerous tumor. His team made an exact copy of the patient's windpipe from a porous, fibrous plastic. This plastic windpipe was then seeded with stem cells harvested from the patient's bone marrow. The seeded windpipe was grown in a lab, then transplanted into the patient. Fifteen months after the operation, the patient was tumor-free and tests revealed the new windpipe was developing a blood vessel network. As Macchiarini explained to the *New York Times*, he would ultimately prefer to get rid of the plastic scaffold and instead have drugs that would enable the body to rebuild its own scaffold. "Don't touch the patient. Just use his body to recreate his own organ. It would be fantastic."[7]

On average, transplant surgeons devote approximately 16 years to education and training. Male surgeons report an average of 15.5 years of training, while female surgeons report 16.6 years. [8]

The creation of a windpipe from a patient's own cells marks an early achievement in the journey toward lab-created organs of all kinds.

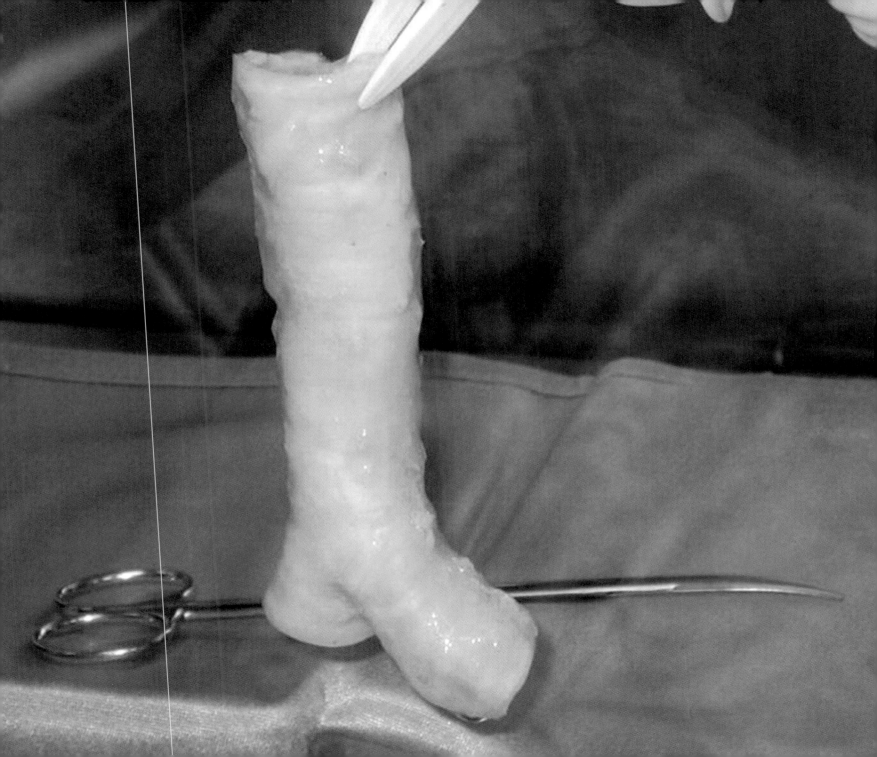

+ Ethical Concerns

White has stated he believes the ethical opposition to head transplant surgery has been seen with other types of transplants in the past: "At each stage—kidney, heart, liver and so forth—ethical considerations have been considered, especially with the heart, which was a major, major problem for many people and scientists." Still, White's work was criticized by other doctors. One remarked, "I cannot see any medical grounds for doing this. . . . And I think that the experiments are the sort that are wholly unethical and inappropriate for any possible reason."[9]

Head and Brain

There is still part of the body that has not been transplanted, partly because it is so complex, but also because many find the idea disturbing: the head and brain. As bizarre as the idea might seem, the idea of head or whole body transplants has been discussed since the early 1900s. Since a brain cannot function without all the intricate blood vessels and nerves that are part of the head, a brain transplant is not in the foreseeable future. However, whole head transplants might be possible.

In the late 1990s, neurosurgeon Dr. Robert White of Case Western Reserve University promoted the idea of whole body transplants for quadriplegics. He noted quadriplegics often die young of multiple organ failure and argued if surgeons could transfer the healthy body of a donor to the healthy head of the quadriplegic, the recipient's life would be prolonged. The operation itself

The delicate, complex connections between the brain and the rest of the body mean brain transplants are unlikely to be successful.

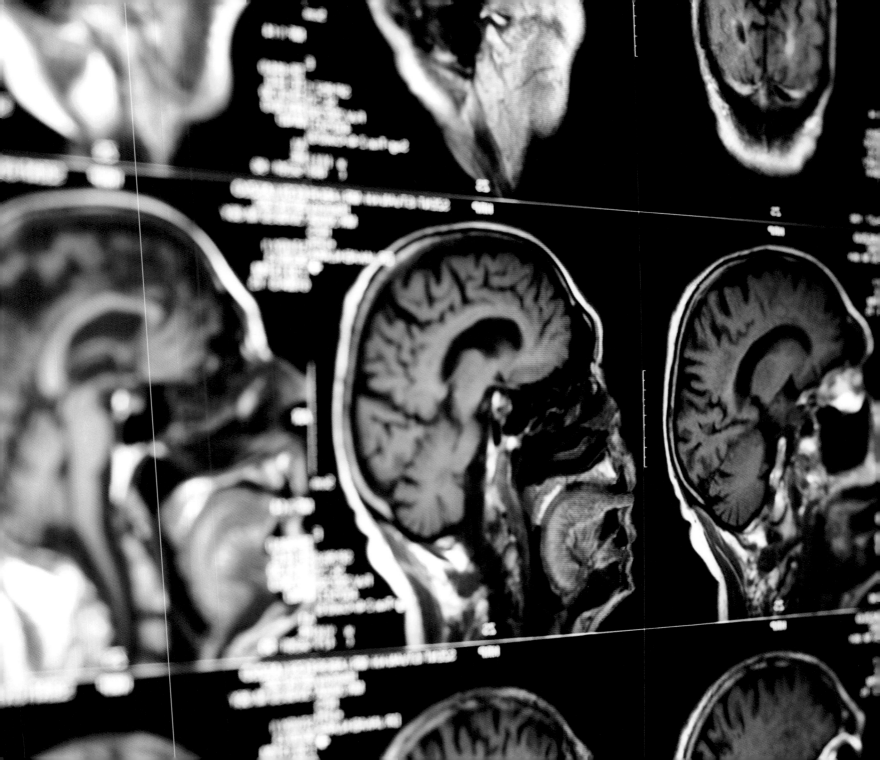

is conceivable because it only involves structures in the neck. In the 1970s, White proved it could be technically accomplished when he transplanted the head of one monkey onto the body of another. But some bioethicists believe the ethical issues surrounding head transplants are so insurmountable it will never happen.

Whole brain transplants also seem unlikely. Scientists are focusing brain transplant research on engineering small pieces of brain tissue, not transplanting a donor brain or growing a whole new brain. They are experimenting with finding out whether small pieces of tissue engineered in a dish can be implanted into small areas of the body and make connections. There is some research showing if stem cells are put in an injured area of the brain, the cells can restore some functionality to the area. It is hoped this kind research might lead to helping patients regain neural function lost to disease or restore a segment of spinal cord function. Growing whole brains is not believed to be on the horizon. But with the incredible advances in transplant research over the last century, scientists know to never say never.

 In the 1950s, Soviet scientists successfully transplanted the head of one dog onto the back of another.

✚ Timeline

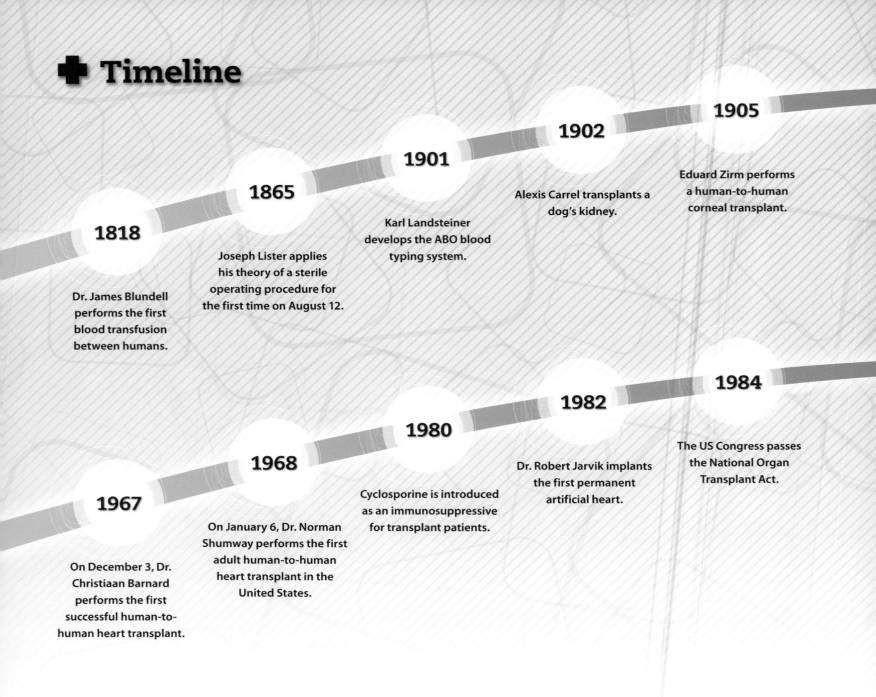

1818

Dr. James Blundell performs the first blood transfusion between humans.

1865

Joseph Lister applies his theory of a sterile operating procedure for the first time on August 12.

1901

Karl Landsteiner develops the ABO blood typing system.

1902

Alexis Carrel transplants a dog's kidney.

1905

Eduard Zirm performs a human-to-human corneal transplant.

1967

On December 3, Dr. Christiaan Barnard performs the first successful human-to-human heart transplant.

1968

On January 6, Dr. Norman Shumway performs the first adult human-to-human heart transplant in the United States.

1980

Cyclosporine is introduced as an immunosuppressive for transplant patients.

1982

Dr. Robert Jarvik implants the first permanent artificial heart.

1984

The US Congress passes the National Organ Transplant Act.

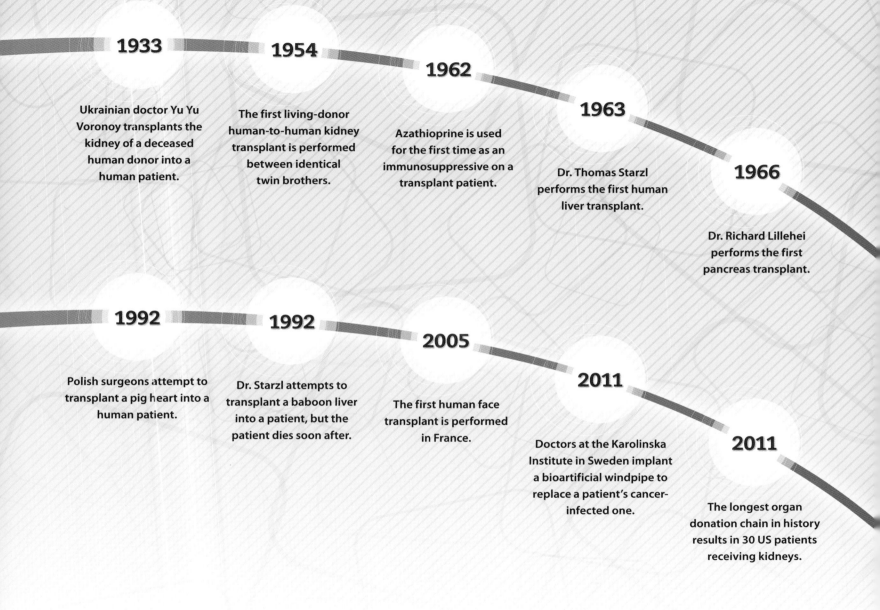

1933

Ukrainian doctor Yu Yu Voronoy transplants the kidney of a deceased human donor into a human patient.

1954

The first living-donor human-to-human kidney transplant is performed between identical twin brothers.

1962

Azathioprine is used for the first time as an immunosuppressive on a transplant patient.

1963

Dr. Thomas Starzl performs the first human liver transplant.

1966

Dr. Richard Lillehei performs the first pancreas transplant.

1992

Polish surgeons attempt to transplant a pig heart into a human patient.

1992

Dr. Starzl attempts to transplant a baboon liver into a patient, but the patient dies soon after.

2005

The first human face transplant is performed in France.

2011

Doctors at the Karolinska Institute in Sweden implant a bioartificial windpipe to replace a patient's cancer-infected one.

2011

The longest organ donation chain in history results in 30 US patients receiving kidneys.

Glossary

allogeneic
Genetically different but belonging to the same species.

amputate
To cut off a projecting body part.

anencephaly
A birth defect resulting in the absence of most of the brain and spinal cord.

anesthetic
A chemical agent that causes loss of sensation either with or without consciousness.

antigen
A foreign substance that enters the body and stimulates the immune system to produce antibodies that target it.

blood vessel
Any of the arteries, veins, and capillaries through which blood circulates in the body.

cyclosporine
An immunosuppressive drug used to prevent the rejection of transplanted organs.

graft
To surgically transplant or implant living tissue into a body to replace damaged tissue or organs.

immunologist

A doctor who studies the immune system.

immunosuppressive

Suppressing the immune response to prevent the rejection of transplants.

prognosis

A prediction of the course and probable outcome of a disease.

stamina

The ability to continue a difficult physical effort.

sterilize

To clean of contamination.

suturing

Surgically closing a wound or joining tissue with a fine thread.

transfusion

To transfer blood or blood products from one individual to another.

xenograft

Cross species tissue or organ transplantation.

Additional Resources

Selected Bibliography

Cooper, David. *Open Heart: The Radical Surgeons Who Revolutionized Medicine*. New York: Kaplan, 2010. Print.

McRae, Donald. *Every Second Counts: The Race to Transplant the First Human Heart*. New York: Penguin, 2006. Print.

Petechuk, David. *Organ Transplantation*. Westport, CT: Greenwood, 2006. Print.

Further Readings

Hunnicutt, Susan C., ed. *Organ Transplants*. Farmington Hills, MI: Greenhaven, 2007. Print.

Marcovitz, Hal. *Organ & Body Donation*. North Mankato, MN: ABDO, 2011. Print.

Web Sites

To learn more about organ transplants, visit ABDO Publishing Company online at **www.abdopublishing.com**. Web sites about organ transplants are featured on our Book Links page. These links are routinely monitored and updated to provide the most current information available.

For More Information

American Organ Transplant Association

PO Box 418
Stilwell, KS 66085
713-344-2402
http://www.aotaonline.org/contact-us.html

Founded in Houston, Texas, by Ellen Woodall in 1986, the American Organ Transplant Association helps transplant centers, patients, and their families with their transportation of organs and resources.

American Society of Transplantation

15000 Commerce Parkway, Suite C
Mount Laurel, NJ 08054
856-439-9986
http://www.a-s-t.org

Founded in 1982, the American Society of Transplantation is comprised of more than 3,000 transplant professionals dedicated to research, education, advocacy, and patient care in transplantation.

Source Notes

Chapter 1. A New Heart

1. "Number of US Transplants Per Year, 1988–2008." *Infoplease*. Pearson Education, 2008. Web. 2 May 2013.

Chapter 2. The Body's Organs

1. "How Many Organs Does a Human Being Have?" *American Association of Anatomists*. American Association of Anatomists, 2012. Web. 2 May 2013.

2. Jane E. Brody. "A Superfluous Organ Can Still Cause Trouble." *New York Times*. New York Times, 16 Nov. 2004. Web. 2 May 2013.

3. "Top 10 Amazing Facts About Your Heart." *LiveScience*. Tech Media Network, 8 Feb. 2007. Web. 2 May 2013.

4. "Lung." *Encyclopaedia Britannica*. Encyclopaedia Britannica, 2013. Web. 2 May 2013.

5. "Kidney, 2011 SRTR & OPTN Annual Data Report." *Scientific Registry of Transplant Recipients*. Health Services and Resources Administration, 2011. Web. 2 May 2013.

6. "Kidney." *Encyclopaedia Britannica*. Encyclopaedia Britannica, 2013. Web. 2 May 2013.

Chapter 3. The Early History of Organ Transplants

1. "Timeline of Important Dates and Events in the Development of Anaesthesia." *History of Anaesthesia Society*. History of Anaesthesia Society, n.d. Web. 4 Feb. 2013.

2. "Lister, Joseph, Baron Lister, Of Lyme Regis." *Encyclopaedia Britannica*. Encyclopaedia Britannica, 2013. Web. 2 May 2013.

Chapter 4. Transplant Successes and Failures

1. "Transplant Pioneers Recall Medical Milestone." *NPR Books*. NPR, 20 Dec. 2004. Web. 4 Feb. 2013.

2. "Kidney-Pancreas Transplant." *National Kidney Foundation*. National Kidney Foundation, 2013. Web. 2 May 2013.

3. David Petechuk. *Organ Transplantation*. Westport, CT: Greenwood, 2006. Print. xi.

Chapter 5. The First Human Heart Transplant

1. Adrian Kantrowitz. "America's First Human Heart Transplantation: The Concept, the Planning, and the Furor." *ASAIO Journal* 44.4 (1998): 251. Print.

Chapter 6. Organ Donations

1. "Statistics." *Donate Life America*. Donate Life America, n.d. Web. 4 Feb. 2013.

2. "Facts." *Global Observatory on Donation & Transplantation*. Spanish National Transplant Organization, 2013. Web. 3 May 2013.

3. "The Gap Continues to Widen." *Organdonor.gov*. US Department of Health and Human Services, n.d. Web. 3 May 2013.

4. "Understanding Donation." *Donate Life America*. Donate Life America, n.d. Web. 4 Feb. 2013.

5. "The Need is Real: Data." *Organdonor.gov*. US Department of Health and Human Services, n.d. Web. 3 May 2013.

6. "Organ Donation: The Process." *Organdonor.gov*. US Department of Health and Human Services, n.d. Web. 3 May 2013.

Chapter 7. Improving Survival Rates

1. "American Society of Transplantation." *Share the Beat*. American Society of Transplantation, 2011. Web. 3 May 2013.

2. "Inventor of the Week Archive: Robert Jarvik." *Lemelson-MIT*. MIT, Apr. 2002. Web. 3 May 2013.

3. "Transplant Innovation and Ethical Challenges: What Have We Learned?" *Cleveland Clinic Journal of Medicine*. Cleveland Clinic Foundation, 2008. Web. 4 Feb. 2013.

4. "Frontline: A History of Xenotransplantation Experiments." *PBS*. PBS, n.d. Web. 4 Feb. 2013.

Source Notes Continued

Chapter 8. Controversy and Challenges

1. Bruce Agnew. "Do We Have the Right to Transplant Animal Parts?" *Snapshots of Science and Medicine.* National Institutes of Health, n.d. Web. 3 May 2013.

2. Ibid.

3. Ibid.

4. Ibid.

5. "Prohibition of Organ Purchases." *Legal Information Institute.* Cornell University Law School, n.d. Web. 3 May 2013.

6. "You're Worth More Dead Than Alive." *MedicalTranscription.net.* MedicalTranscription.net, 2013. Web. 3 May 2013.

7. Denis Campbell and Nicola Davison. "Illegal Kidney Trade Booms As New Organ Is 'Sold Every Hour.'" *Guardian.* Guardian, 27 May 2013. Web. 5 Feb. 2013.

8. Trevor Stokes. "Donating Organs for Cash Sparks Controversy." *Fox News.* Fox News, 28 Sept. 2013. Web. 5 Feb. 2013.

9. Denis Campbell and Nicola Davison. "Illegal Kidney Trade Booms As New Organ Is 'Sold Every Hour.'" *Guardian.* Guardian, 27 May 2013. Web. 5 Feb. 2013.

10. M. R. Marvin, K. M. Prager, M. V. Wohlauer, and J. G. Chandler. "Sanctity and Organ Donation's Societal Value." *Bulletin of the American College of Surgeons* 97.1 (2012). Web. 5 Feb. 2013.

Chapter 9. Transplants Today and Tomorrow

1. "Kidney Transplant." *Encyclopedia of Surgery.* Encyclopedia of Surgery, n.d. Web. 5 Feb. 2013.

2. Alex Radkewycz. "Ten Year Milestone Reached By Lung Transplant Recipient." *Hospital News.* Wall2Wall Media, 14 Feb. 2012. Web. 5 Feb. 2013.

3. "Heart Transplant Survival Rates Improving." *CBC News.* CBC News, 24 Oc. 2011. Web. 5 Feb. 2013.

4. David Petechuk. *Organ Transplantation.* Westport, CT: Greenwood, 2006. Print. 10.

5. "University of Maryland Patient Exceeding Expectations Seven Months After Most Extensive Face Transplant Ever Performed." *University of Maryland Medical Center.* University of Maryland, 16 Oct. 2012. Web. 5 Feb. 2013.

6. Kevin Sack. "60 Lives, 30 Kidneys, All Linked." *New York Times.* New York Times, 18 Feb. 2012. Web. 3 May 2013.

7. Henry Fountain. "A First: Organs Tailor-Made With Body's Own Cells." *New York Times.* New York Times, 15 Sept. 2012. Web. 3 May 2013.

8. L. S. Florence, et al. "Academic Careers and Lifestyle Characteristics of 171 Transplant Surgeons in the ASTS." *American Journal of Transplantation* 11.2 (2011): 261–271. Web. 5 Feb. 2013.

9. "Frankenstein Fears After Head Transplant." *BBC News.* BBC, 6 Apr. 2001. Web. 3 May 2013.

Index

Index Continued

About the Author

Racquel Foran is a freelance writer living in Coquitlam, British Columbia, Canada. She enjoys writing about politics, current events, and social issues and is a frequent contributor to magazines and newspapers in her region.

About the Consultant

Susan E. Lederer, PhD, is the Robert Turell Professor in History of Medicine and Bioethics at the University of Wisconsin School of Medicine and Public Health. Her books include *Subjected to Science: Human Experimentation in America Before the Second World War* (Johns Hopkins University Press, 1995); *Frankenstein: Penetrating the Secrets of Nature* (Rutgers University Press, 2002), and *Flesh and Blood: A Cultural History of Transplantation and Transfusion in Twentieth-Century America* (Oxford University Press, 2008).